BOOK III

DECODING DIS-EASE

METAPHYSICAL INTERPRETATION

O.M. KELLY

COPYRIGHT

Copyright © 2023 Margret Ann Kelly/O.M. Kelly
Series: Book III (Revised)
First Published as Book III in "Decoding the Mind of God",
Margret Ann Kelly/O.M. Kelly, Copyright © 2011.
ISBN: 978-0-6452492-5-5

All rights reserved. This book may not be reproduced, wholly or in part, or transmitted in any form whatsoever without written permission from the author, O.M. Kelly, www.elanea.com.

The author of this book does not dispense medical advice or prescribe the use of any technique as a form of treatment for physical, emotional, or medical problems without the advice of a physician, either directly or indirectly. The intent of the author is only to offer information of a general nature to help you in your quest for emotional and spiritual well-being. In the event you use any of the information in this book for yourself, which is your constitutional right, the author assumes no responsibility for your actions.

AUTHOR

Author O. M. Kelly, known as Omni to her clients and students is an accomplished author and international lecturer, on Metaphysics, Philosophy and understanding the Collective Consciousness. Omni consults for Member States of the European Commission as a Conciliation Advisor and Rhetoric Counsellor for other International Companies throughout Europe. Omni now resides on Australia's beautiful Gold Coast, writing books, and works as a Life Mentor and Business Coach.

Omni has dedicated her life to decoding the mysteries of the universe. With a deep knowledge of the biblical agenda, mythologies including ancient Egyptology, Asian principles, and metaphysical insights, Omni has discovered the secret that all stories share a coded hidden metaphysical language. Her seminal work, "Decoding the Mind of God", is a compilation of nine volumes of metaphysical information based on the research into the coded information of the Laws of the Universe, also known as the Collective Consciousness, and represents a groundbreaking contribution to our understanding of the metaphysical universe. Now, all nine volumes are being released as separate, revised books, each offering a unique perspective on the universe's workings. Omni's work has been widely acclaimed for its depth of insight, and her contributions to the field of metaphysics have been groundbreaking.

THIS BOOK

Introducing "Decoding Dis-Ease" a Metaphysical Interpretation into understanding the intricate web of factors that contribute to our health and well-being. From the author of several groundbreaking works on the interaction of the mind and body, this book delves into a wide range of topics related to dis-ease. It is a fascinating and insightful book that offers a fresh perspective on health and healing. It is a must-read for anyone interested in the mind-body connection.

Readers will be inspired to embark on a quest of discovering the codes within themselves, recognizing that every cell in our body is pure Cosmic Consciousness. They will also gain a deeper understanding of specific health topics such as the thyroid, the kidneys, men's problems, and many other topics from a Metaphysical perspective. The book also examines how a dis-ease is given to us in group energy and the complex interplay between our bodies and minds, and how every human has the consequences of all that we do and experience.

CONTENT

Introduction

Chapter One
Every Human Has The Consequences Of All
Dis-Eases Known To Man — Page 1

Chapter Two
Cancer — Page 8

Chapter Three
Parasites Within The Body — Page 11

Chapter Four
The Holographic Enchantment Of Thought — Page 13

Chapter Five
How A Dis-Ease Is Given To Us In Group Energy — Page 14

Chapter Six
God And The Unconscious Mind At Work — Page 18

Chapter Seven
The Quest Of Discovering The Codes Within You — Page 21

Chapter Eight
A Cell Is Pure Cosmic Consciousness — Page 30

Chapter Nine
The HIV/AIDS Virus — Page 34

Chapter Ten
The Mind Of The Pedophile — Page 42

Chapter Eleven
Our Responsibilities — Page 44

Chapter Twelve
Dis-Ease, Cancer, And The Thyroid — Page 49

Chapter Thirteen
Intellectual Disability — Page 55

Chapter Fourteen We Program Our Children's Desires, Expectations, And Future Inheritance	Page 60
Chapter Fifteen The Kidneys	Page 66
Chapter Sixteen The Obese Child	Page 69
Chapter Seventeen Understanding Our Intelligence	Page 71
Chapter Eighteen Viruses	Page 75
Chapter Nineteen War	Page 78
Chapter Twenty Body Language	Page 83
Chapter Twenty One The Dis-Ease You Create	Page 87
Chapter Twenty Two The Temple Mind	Page 97
Chapter Twenty Three Love Is The Oracle Of Life	Page 101
Chapter Twenty Four Men's Problems	Page 104
Chapter Twenty Five Thoughts	Page 107
Books by O.M. Kelly (Omni)	Page 110

INTRODUCTION

This book has changed my entire perspective on illness. It took me years to connect to the importance of how we promote and collect each dis-ease; slowly, I began to understand how it was expressed back to us, and then I could not set aside the book I was writing. I just wanted to keep on writing and writing. The question-and-answer section is interesting, and it details my explanations as to how we inherit our dis-eases through the generations of the family.

I also came to understand how this energy runs through our body, collecting the negative reproach we allow ourselves to create that these dis-eases build up in the body through the mathematics of the mind harmonizing and rebalancing the emotional responses that have been detained; in other words, through the ego searching for its own quarry.

Every dis-ease on this planet—whether it be cancer, aids, diabetes, etc., right down to the common cold—has been collected through the distinction of our emotional responses recording our thinking.

I have now accepted how pain is created in the body, and the reason why the mind must alert the body to where and how our thoughts are taking us along for the ride.

The blessings come when you can set yourself a challenge to return your mind back to self—to view every thought you are repeating again and again!
Omni

CHAPTER ONE

Every Human Has The Consequences Of All Dis-Eases Known To Man

This book will change your entire perspective about illness. I found that I did not want to end it; I just wanted to keep on writing. When I thought I had finished, more information came through each time I reread my words.

As you read, you will learn to understand how we inherit our dis-eases through the generations of our family. You will be given an explanation as to how the dis-eases build up through each generation conforming to their emotions, and then how we innocently pass that responsibility on to the mind of the next generation. The question-and-answer section explains the challenges that most people have regarding the huge responsibility of accepting their dis-ease – and also explains how they can deal with all this.

A dis-ease is created through our thought patterns, and our cells react according to how we are relating to each thought we think. Our energy runs through the body to create the dis-ease that must build up in us, through the mathematics of the mind harmonizing and rebalancing our emotional responses that we have innocently allowed to be detained through the ego searching for its own quarry.

The book explains how we can begin to heal our dis-ease, through being alerted to our thinking and pulling ourselves up before the responses can begin to habituate in the mind; even the rampant dis-eases threatening the planet as a whole, each of which has a life sentence attached to it. By changing our thinking, we can begin to realize, through balancing our mind, just how easy it could be for all mankind to release the self-imposed punishment of not releasing the inner self.

That energy runs through our body to create dis-eases like cancer, aids, and diabetes etc., right down to the common cold or even a broken fingernail – through the distinction of our emotional responses in regard to our thinking. You will learn to accept how pain is created in the body, and the reason why the mind must alert the body about just where your thoughts are taking you.

Before you become too involved in this book, may I say to you that I will not become delusive and make an excuse for the words that you are about to read. This information has taken many years to bring together, and not one detriment is attached to any person who has a dis-ease – implying such is by no means my intension. I am merely explaining to you the next intellectual step of humanity's awareness. You are receiving my wits – which are my Wisdom, Intelligence, Truth and my Soul– of how I have understood and earned my education. So, if you become affected or afflicted through your readings, please remember to take heed of this paragraph. Release the monkey off your shoulders, and open your heart to yourself in order to be able to receive your gift of attaining eternal life. Hopefully, in future editions, I can remove this paragraph and replace it with another earning, not another yearning.

Hopefully by now, you are becoming more aware of the Metaphysical language embedded in your genes and how it automatically filters throughout your body. This language has always been in its rightful place; it is just that you have not been aware of it until now. For you to pick up this book you are hoping to become more aware of yourself and the hesitancy of learning more about this inner self that we cannot see, and as you know it is hidden in plain sight. It stems from within and grows according to your thinking.

A dis-ease is an adversary to the fact that the human conditions of thought are searching for and beyond the plurality of the mind.

The introduction to the word disease ("dis-ease") – and the results of that word, through understanding the Metaphysical language – is brought to our attention with the connection as to how we can evolve up into the intelligence of the unconscious mind. When our attention is brought to a dis-ease, we find that it is created through the results of our

DNA, which is triggered in us through the past thoughts of the inheritance we have received from our forefathers and our parents. Once we fully understand this sentence, we can become more aware of our moment, which, in time, will allow your future to return to you! The unconscious mind harbours every thought we think, and, slowly, through some of us entering up into this sphere of intelligence, we can help you understand your next evolutionary step.

This inheritance is through the worlds of our past thoughts, our intelligence – or our "Intel-Legiance" – that we create with self. That word represents our inner computer, which has the responsibility of bringing the program of self together, and which enhances the correct behavioural patterns that coerce with the everlasting energy. Our intelligence is released only through learning to trust and earning belief in self.

Every human has the consequences of all dis-ease known to man. It makes no difference who or why you are, and it does not judge you; a dis-ease just applies and attaches itself through the thought that you have allowed to rule as a result of a personality of self that overrides a positive behaviour. The results begin to empower a dis-ease that is equivalent to that thought, through the source piling up through the Collective Consciousness. How and what you think segregates the mind into its own tribes, creating the Laws of Self. It feels that it has earned the priority right to rule. This is where it becomes your responsibility to become totally aware of each thought that is blindly running around in your head.

The stories of the twelve tribes of Israel in the Bible are also an explanation of our emotional responses, which create the scenes of the worlds we will mostly habituate and become. This is for the pleasure of the consequences that we use for our own self-satisfaction. It starts with a flush, which then becomes a blush, and then the scene is set for the play to begin.

A dis-ease is set in motion through a viral attitude towards self or others. Any dis-ease that we create is a thought regarding an embarrassing situation that we have allowed to build-up and have prescribed it to our self.

An embarrassing situation is where we automatically (self-governing) wish to hide behind our thinking – all through us believing that no one is listening; and, through the Collective Consciousness, which we call 'God' or the 'Greatest Oracle of the Divine', or alternatively the 'Laws of the Universe', they are all too soon brought back to our attention. That embarrassing situation begins to create the word shame, which is brought through the codes of language into our understanding, and the energy from that word must be returned back into our Collective Intelligence.

The word shame is created for the value of the kidneys, in order to keep them functioning, unhindered, for their own self-worth. This is also where the word void comes from. When we cannot void – or pass – our urine, the waters of consciousness are backed up in our body, and it becomes ashamed of the excuses that we are making in response to our self.

The unconscious mind is measuring every move that we make through every thought we think, and if we fall out of alignment through our inner personalities not measuring up to what we are thinking. Bang! The Collective of self – or the unconscious mind –then announces its intension. This then explains to the kidneys just what their responsibility must uphold. They have a working program where they must seat themselves with the government of this wonderful form of energy that we call our human body.

This begins to affect the sensitivity of the endocrine system, which is the first system to become afflicted when the body has a lesson to learn. The water must flow; it must not become stagnant through our closing the doors of our house. Are you beginning to understand a little more of how I am expressing the Metaphysical language to you?

The endocrine system holds the responsibility of the childish attitude that we sometimes use when we find an excuse for not following up on our thoughts. As it registers with the unconscious mind, it builds and collects itself through its own negative attitude; it begins to become overloaded. The next system then feels this pulse and, in turn, it applies for the position to help release that pressure. This is the responsibility of the immune system, which brings out the warriors within to fight the overlord that the dis-ease has created for itself. It tries not to overload the body anymore. As the energy of that dis-ease is beginning to become more condensed and powerful, it puts up a good fight with the immune system.

If both forces cannot come to a conclusion, the game continues. The dis- ease begins to register and build upon itself, until the lymphatic system – or what is also known as the united "overlord" of the nervous system – must confront the overlord of the pending dis-ease. If the thoughts that created the dis-ease are not being addressed by you, the lymphatic system must surrender to the dis-ease. Once this system is affected, our hope of resurrection begins to dwindle, and we collapse in stature. All through you harbouring a past experience that bruised your ego!

We can compare this game to the movie Star Wars. A short digression here for the moment. I have been informed that George Lucas, the creator of Star Wars, undertook training under the guidance of the late brilliant author Joseph Campbell, who wrote more than sixty books and gave us a wealth of information that he had gathered from around the world regarding the Masks of God.

When George Lucas had gathered his information, he sat down and wrote the magnificent Star Wars series that is still so popular today. All his movies can be taken as exercises explaining the emotional personalities of the mind, and these personalities are just a spark of what is in each human for to view for him/herself. Luke Skywalker had to find his strength in order to release his light, and he did so through over-coming the dark force – Darth Vader. The secret of the movie came that at the end, when Luke found out that the dark force was really his father. In other words, he had the responsibility of clearing his past evolution – or DNA – of its own negativity, and only then was he free to collect what he needed to experience for himself.

Now back to the explanation of dis-ease. Having defeated the lymphatic system, the dis-ease is in all its glory. All this time it has fed off the original childish attitude that has, over time, grown into something more viral than what you started with.

It has been looked after and fed with encouragement to grow and prosper in its self-worth, through you not attending to the original thought. That lack of attention allowed the dis-ease to continue pulsing away.

It is only when you become aware of your thinking and begin to change your mind that the dis-ease has the opportunity to be brought back to your attention. This is always in the right moment, at the right time, depending on the depth of your thinking and how long you want to keep this past experience under your own control.

Your doctor may inform you that you are on the way to creating something greater within your system; he/she is alerted to the build-up of the forthcoming dis-ease through the symptoms that you are registering back to him. Pay attention to your mind! You cannot give this dis-ease to anyone else! It has become your own responsibility totally! Through your innocence of not adjusting your thinking, you have earned it.

We now realize that we must accept this new dis-ease, as it is the results of its own creation through our repetitious thinking. We place this responsibility through the depressed thought, and that depressed thought begins by you overloading and pressurizing yourself with the same excuse over and over again. This alerts just one cell, and that cell then builds upon itself and begins to pulse and coagulate into its own energy. It creates its own life force. It keeps itself alive from the energy of you living in your past, and it repeats itself time after time after time.

Through its power building and igniting itself into its own strength, that cell then alerts other cells which feel the pulse of that cell, and then they rush to relate to it. If that cell is inflamed through its anger, the emotion begins to change, and it builds itself up and into the emotion of "Hate". The other cells are alerted to the strength of this cell, and they rush to its aid – and, if they are not strong enough, they are automatically consumed by this wisdom. That wisdom is the wise emotion that has reached its own zenith. Hopefully, through reading these last few paragraphs, you can understand that what I am explaining to you is one of the largest dis-eases we have created – the one that we have named cancer.

Your Notes:

CHAPTER TWO

Cancer

Cancer is an energy that takes around ten years to manifest into its own light. If it is not brought to its own attention, it grows beyond its own recognition before it moves up into the knowledge of the lymphatic system.

So, when you are given the results of your tests through your doctor, discovering that cancer is imminent or has already occurred, you my friend, have just been given your ultimate challenge – all through the right hemisphere of your brain finally being able to step forward to support every thought you think! This becomes a blessing for the ego to receive, to give it the opportunity to conform through its own grace.

Your emotional kingdoms are your supreme ruler, and, through an open heart, your courage also steps forward to realign you with a positive attitude, where you have the opportunity to look back through the past ten years of your life. By looking back into your thoughts of the past, you will begin to see the progressive behaviour of your thinking, and what you have allowed yourself to create through constantly repeating the bitterness of your past thoughts.

Each stage of cancer grows collectively over the years, and, on the place where that cancer began, determines what part it can claim from your body. It chooses exactly the right section that has not been homogenized; i.e., the organ that has had superior mind control over others. It is impelled into each area through your unconscious mind. If your parents never overcame their fear, that fear is autonomically instilled through your DNA, and this homogeny is then heralded back to you. The unconscious mind is continually shouting to you, "Enough is enough!" That message is coming from your Soul mind – your God Force – which is the highest realms of intellect.

I will not make any excuses for my story; I myself had cancer over thirty years ago. I had been given the death sentence, and then decided to enquire and learn more about this disease. I began to become more aware of the excuses I had made through not having the confidence to know myself; I could see the path that I had created, or allowed to manifest on my behalf, in order to deliver unto me the results of my actions. It was not a nice time, as I began to recall my anger.

The most important learning for me was to understand that I had not realized how long that cancer had been slowly building up into its own perfection or wisdom. It had begun years earlier, when all my children were young, and I had to face the responsibility of rearing them on my own. I was running our property alone while my husband worked away from home; anything that had to be done around the property and the home was totally my responsibility.

I found my anger growing, as I had no one to share this burden with. There were cows to milk, pigs to feed, and lucerne to grow, water, cut, and bale. There were chickens, ducks, turkeys, and geese by the hundreds, and they seemed to multiply very quickly. We had built up quite a menagerie. This anger – and hatred – that I felt had built up of its own accord, and, day by day, it had grown more vicious. The time came when I began to ostracize myself; by that I mean, I could no longer feel my own existence. The words "faith in self" were pushed further back into my inner dictionary, and I felt like I was losing the responsibility to even accept them.

From those words, I learned that, through us depending on our own weakness, our Higher Self urges us to bring our faith out to stand alongside us so that we can learn to accept the potentiality of those words and bring them into our heart, not leave them tucked away in our vocabulary. I realized that the two words fate and faith were a counterbalance of one another. Our fate will keep on controlling us until we begin to accept our faith within.

Food was plentiful at our place, and the table was always piled high, so we could feed our own family tribe and the eleven other tribes as well. My eldest children learned responsibility very early in their life. They became my backbone and could support me with their strength as I tottered on the brink of my own demise. I look back now and wonder how I had ever completed my tasks.

My journey with cancer is now by forty - six years past. Not long ago, I had a check-up from my general practitioner, who told me that even with my weak heart, which I had been born with, I had the bodily functions of a woman in her mid-twenties, and, seeing that I am now beginning my eighties, I have accepted and congratulated myself for a job well done! Did you know that in my land – Australia – the statistics state that one in three people will create their own cancer? We are only two hundred years old, and our population has been attained through people from other countries migrating, all through them wanting to improve themselves!

Each cell is a Collective Memory of the Soul – or Collective Inheritance of the DNA – and has the power to build itself into its own accreditation through the strength that we have given it. Every cell in our body is a photographic response to each thought we think! It does not matter which dis-ease it is or what name we give it; it becomes an emotion within our body that is continually walking backwards, looking to be excused.

A final thought for us to think regarding the applicability of contracting cancer through other sources is the Chernobyl disaster, radiation poisoning, as well as the animal species. Not everyone perished, but those who did were unconsciously measured through the Collective Inheritance of all; this was through their Collective Consciousness vibrating to the same frequency of the mathematics of radiation. We call that "innocence". The fallout from that radiation has interrupted the flow of the next generation, all through us still not having learned.

Your Notes:

CHAPTER THREE

Parasites Within The Body

Let us now venture into the world of parasites and how they are naturally created in the body. This type of thinking creates a storm in the home of bacterial responses, which is where our viral infections begin, and which creates a parasitic indulgence with the thought in the moment. A parasite is first created in the bowel, and its life force is fed through our continual reflections of holding onto past experiences; as a result, it thrives at the expense of our thinking. Believe me it has plenty of places to hide.

Your faeces are the creation of the faces or masks that you hide behind – that which has become trapped through your past thinking. This is the Metaphysical explanation of constipation; it is the holding onto yesterday's thinking, and the refusal to let it go or take the responsibility to acknowledge it. That memory is also the creation of facial paralysis, which is the precursor to all strokes. When you are trapped back into your primal energy, you are living off your faeces, or the faces that you are wearing, and bastardizing your thoughts back to your own Higher Self. Your face registers all this, and then it must contort through to the unconscious mind.

Thus, when we have digested our thoughts, the energy is supposed to filter throughout the body, and then release into the bowel; but, if our thoughts have not been stored correctly, the brain becomes overloaded, where it has to take on extra responsibility, which, in turn, deters our achievements.

Remember that the brain and bowel are related to each other in self- worthiness, through the Soul or unconscious mind. The brain stores our future, and the bowel stores our past; it is a bipolar activation that creates the dynamo effect. This is announcing the same desire that we see with the new dis-ease we have named "bipolar disorder". The moment my attention was alerted regarding this dis-ease, the patients began to come for consultancy. I was surprised at the split personalities they had created for themselves. They were the child in one instance and tried to be the adult in the next! And, as the adult realized the strength it was creating for itself, it then ostracized and ordered back to the child; again the ego was refusing to allow itself to grow into its next step. The dynamo effect is characterized by two opposing opinions: one is the majority, and the other is the minority. Once I had mastered this dis-ease of the mind, I rearranged my thinking as to how I could assist my client by explaining to them, their insecurities in facing up to themselves in each moment, as they watched their tide change into a more positive and peaceful behaviour.

Your Notes:

CHAPTER FOUR

The Holographic Enchantment Of Thought

We have the ideal opportunity to create and manifest the eggs of parasites. They are the result of the unconscious recognition of self. Yes, that's a shock!! Please don't blame the animals for your parasites. If you are trapped in your past – which is also your animal thinking or primal mind – and you have sucked your mind down into those lower thoughts, these parasites have been given the free reign to manifest. It is their right to feel at home. Just being in the same room with someone you detest triggers these responses to activate through the Collective Consciousness. It is the self, re-creating the self. Parasites are the creation of our thoughts explaining a thought in reverse through to our eternalness; which is only through the mind living the same excuses being replayed over and over again.

Through the holographic enchantment of thought, the parasite is created through the expense of the emotion that you are living in, and it finds its home base; it must manifest in those conditions. It breeds in multiples of millions, as that thought independently becomes a stronger life force that continually repeats and expands throughout the cells. The cells are in overload. The parasites then gather together and become their own kingdom; they join forces with one another into their own oneness, and they grow larger. The body is out of the natural communication with self, and it has to work overtime to keep up its habitual energy. Different types of parasitic worms like to invade our human form. The minute worms like to find their host in the upper tract of our body, where our thoughts are released from the mind. The larger worms like to embed themselves in the stomach and upper intestines. Still-larger worms like to travel down and hook into the lower intestines. The body has become the host nation through the insecurity of that person's thinking, and these parasites flourish in warm, moist conditions. If the body becomes overheated through our thoughts that have not been released, those parasitic worms have the opportunity to rule supreme.

CHAPTER FIVE

How A Dis-Ease Is Given To Us In Group Energy

Years ago, when I commenced my training into the world of Metaphysical language, I asked for my journey to be released to me step by step. "That is no problem," God said. "This is exactly how everything is released to every one of you, in every moment of your lives, whether you are aware of it or not." That shut me up!

I began to see how a dis-ease is given to us in group energy, and my realization began with the research into the Ebola virus, which was prevalent at that time. I asked why only a certain amount of people with that dis-ease had to die in each village, while others lived. If these villages were isolated, why were some people allowed to live? How was the dis-ease carried down the river and passed on to the next village, where only a few died, and then again passed on to the village after that, and so on? I went through all the codes as to how many people had died in each village compared to how the message had been delivered. I always came up with the same answer: "The mind marries the mind." It took quite a few months for me to understand and accept this wisdom that it is, as it should be.

It was according to how the tribe emitted their ego and emotions to one another as to who gathered the virus to themselves. It was passed on as same mind to same mind; like attracts like. Who died in the village was the responsibility of the Elder of the tribe, as well as the conditions that he warranted for the law of the village to understand and abide by.

Through wanting to extend my research, I began to see it all happening in my own village. This began to present itself to me through the customers who came into our restaurant on Sundays, after church services, to have their midday meal. Eating after church, they returned home feeling fulfilled with their morning.

This was correlated over a two-year period, and I can laugh to myself now as I recall one of these stories. In one section sat the Baptists, and in another section were the Jehovah's Witnesses. The Catholics sat over by the window, and the Church of England followers sat in the far corner. And many others came and went. I had thought that my restaurant was a unified heaven for all of them to sit in and share their conversations. At that time, I was studying the philosophies of Buddhism, so we had a global gathering of religions every Sunday. I would meet them at the entrance and guide them to their seats; There are times when I felt like St Peter at the pearly gates!

You know that joke, don't you, about the time God came to check out the scene in heaven? He met a flush-faced Peter at the gates and said, "What is going on here Peter? I can't see anyone in my heavenly abode; you seemed to have put up all these fences. What are they here for? There should be one big united light here for all the world to see, not all these little beams trying to shine out of the heavens. This is our heavenly Paradise, and it is called the Promised Land for all to live in harmony. What is going on? Why are they here?"

Peter hurriedly replied, "Well, Lord, this section over here is for the Catholics, behind that fence there are the Jehovah's Witnesses, and over there are the Buddhists. On the other side of the fence are the Jews, and if you come across here with me, I will show you around all the other sections."

"But why are the fences here, Peter?" God said. Peter replied, "I had to put the fences up, Sir, to keep the peace. This way, they think they are the only ones here!!"

Let us return to the story. Sundays in our restaurant were roast dinner days. You had the choice of roast beef, lamb, chicken, or pork, and crackling. Why would they want to go home and cook for the whole family, when we could serve it exquisitely to them at an economical price, and with no washing up for them to do afterwards? This was their day out. My husband kept very busy in the kitchen, and he served them all through his perfection. I wandered around and made sure that they were satisfied, and, of course, their conversations turned to, "How are you keeping?" It came as quite a shock when I started to realize that many of the people who were members of the same religion contracted the same dis-ease. I remember one group in which nine women contracted the same dis-ease within nine months of each other. The dis-ease was endometriosis, which is created through an inner crying – and all through their lack of achieving their sexual satisfaction – and which is also the precursor to Diabetes.

There were five in another group who all contracted cancer within the same twelve months; four women had breast cancer, and one man had testicular cancer. Both dis-eases are in relationship to one another, through the bitterness they harboured regarding self and others. They all played cards together one night a month.

In another group, were three who contracted lupus, which is created through the refusal to accept and nourish the self, and also the refusal to produce new ideas. Three young women were the mothers of children with Down's syndrome children, which meant that their minds had been set on not having children. Seven from another faith – four men and three women – each had given in to the program of diabetes.

Here were the codes again, introducing me to another aspect of the Laws of the Universe – or God's exclusive consciousness. I had to understand, through the sacredness of the numbers, just what the hidden message was. I had to understand how each dis-ease began to collect itself. What were they thinking that allowed those dis-eases to coincide with each religion – and also, most importantly, what did they believe in?

I learned to understand why each dis-ease was committed to just one religion, and why those dis-eases weren't mixed evenly amongst all faiths. I found that it is not according to the way we are living; it goes further back than that. It is the way our ego overrides the emotional thoughts that try to correspond with one another – which is all delivered up to the unconscious mind – that sets the ball rolling. This derivative factor from the Hidden God was again presenting itself to me.

Then I had to step up my own ladder and learn to understand

the next level: How the Divine energy created itself as a legacy for the planet to inherit in order for us to earn and overcome. As my intellect was opening up, I began to notice the colours that were being referenced through their aura, and I realized that each dis-ease created its own hue. All of which is an outer cry that releases from the body, and this is delivered to us from the unconscious mind. The numbers were coming to the forefront with each case.

Your Notes:

CHAPTER SIX

God And The Unconscious Mind At Work

In one area that I had previously lived in, a group of eleven young men from different faiths and tribes – all of whom were under eighteen years of age – contracted the dis-ease of leukemia and died within four months of one another. This was an interesting case to my sciential (to know the knowing) mind, and I wanted to go into the unravelling this phenomenon. So, again, I began to research the mind of the dis-ease. Each quest I took on was advancement over the previous one.

Five of those young men came from all walks of life among local families, and they had lived there for most of their lives. The other six had moved to the area from somewhere else. One family had moved into the area from the north eighteen months before. Two families had moved from the east, seven and nine months before, respectively. Another family had moved from the south six months before, and the last two families had arrived from the west in the previous four months. They had journeyed for thousands of kilometres, to come into this area. They were highly intellectual and not abusive to their way of life. These were young, intelligent minds. What was their penance to remind humanity in regard to what was happening around the area? Or was it a penance? These young boys were on the next level of their education and had taken up apprenticeships or had accepted and had gone on to the higher levels of university. Who were these Masters, who volunteered to explain to the area, what we were in the process of awakening to become a future detriment to the area.

To begin with, I realized that I was presented with the Medicine Wheel of directions here, and I knew that I had to go within – to search the Cosmos – for the explanation to understand the unconscious energy at work.

The meanings of the different directions are: North: Message from above. East: Message from within. South: Message from the past. West: Dichotomy; where we bring the energy of both hemispheres of our brain into harmonizing with one another.

What message were these young men to deliver to the area? Why did they have to sojourn overland to die together? What was the mass of Collective Consciousness trying to return to us? It was a shock to the whole area, and this tragedy brought the people together. They began to look around in order to place the blame on something – or someone – else, and, finally, they settled on the spray that was used to support the crops. Over time, the chemical company changed its formula, which was unconsciously the result of the message as to why they all had to die. Here was my gathering point. I had to reach up into the Alchemy of the mind to view the measurements of the mathematics between the chemicals used and the chemicals of that group of young men, who had formed their own small collective.

The Collective Mind had colluded, or collided, with the higher minds of each of them. This was a reimbursement handed down and delivered back to us, and the dis-ease of their small collective of energy began to fit the bill. Five of the young men were locals, and the other six had to bring their energy into the area in order to collect the mathematics needed so that we could learn and earn for the entire community. The number five (5) represents the emotion of "freedom", and the number six (6) represents the emotion of "gathering to master oneself", so these wonderful young men had gathered together to wake the area up as to the dangers of the spray. The reason for their age was through the number eighteen (18), which is nearly three cycles of seven. You see how the numbers are God's work! These young men were the forerunners of the future derangement of that area. The number one (1) is reflected to us as the "I am", the number eight (8) is reflected to us as harmony and balance; it also represents the word infinity. When we add these two numbers together, we reach the number nine (9), which represents symbolic death.

I salute these young men, who were Masters in their own right to warn us of what could have been an impending disaster for many other innocent people. This is God and the unconscious mind at work, and it is happening every day somewhere on the planet; we have to set the story straight, and accept that there are always reasons to our seasons.

Your Notes:

CHAPTER SEVEN

The Quest Of Discovering The Codes Within You

I wish to speak to those of you who have a commitment to the quest of discovering the codes within you; which means those of you who are accepting this next dimension of humanity's earnings. Some people refer to this education as the -alternative- way; through others using that word, it is only to satisfy their ego, where they are afraid to accept their own reprimand. My right brain informs me that it is not the alternative; rather, it is the way we have been forced to accept the word, through the control of others, and it differs from the original way. This wonderful word is explaining to us that we are "altering the native within". In other words, we are finally accepting our self and are growing up! It is, and has always been, the next intellectual step to discovering the future of humanity's earnings.

One important factor that is prevalent on the quest is to get through the path of ascension, where we learn to accept who we really are, so that we have a golden opportunity to understand and release these old worlds of our inherited fear. The importance of this next step is to announce to the ego the clarity you will accomplish through reaping the rewards of accepting and becoming your inner sight, which you will so fervently now believe in. All is the directive of our emotional right hemisphere's responsibility of the brain – the worlds of our energy in motion.

Most of you who are being introduced into the language of the Metaphysical, receive the symptoms of meningitis. This has been bestowed upon us, through the changes we have positively created, as we climb up higher into the neural pathways of ascension, which creates this encephalization effect – much the same way as that which the dolphin and whale species have created for themselves through the millennia of their own evolution. They live permanently in the unconscious energy. Remember, this is how the language of the Bible was written and collected in ancient times.

This dis-ease of recorded memory is automatically swathed in layers of protection, which the hypothalamus gland has created through our past generations when expectancies were not measured and accounted for correctly. Can you, the medical apprentices and practitioners of the future, now begin to understand how each dis-ease begins to collect itself?

Our retainers had reached their zenith. That gland appears as cyst-like structures; hence, the difficulty we have as we birth through the eternal obligations in order to be accepted up into the unconscious mind. In other words, our predecessors had been reimbursed for their dues, and the responsibility for this immense challenge is automatically passed on to you. We are now more aware of how each dis-ease has the opportunity to improve upon its own behaviour, through the past thought that houses and protects our ultimate fear. Through the language of the codes, the symptoms of this energy are our own multiple personalities learning to understand and release the hold that our ego won't allow or refuses to transform. The inner primal fear, as we know it, is very protective of its own territory, and it tries to ward us off.

For those of you who have not yet succumbed to this next step, maybe now you can understand the reasoning behind your stiff neck and shoulders, which we know is the ego's stubborn rejection to your inner wisdom. You are carrying too much responsibility – just like Atlas, you have the world on your shoulders. When your belief in self builds upon its own strength and creates your next positive thought, your life becomes so much easier for you to manage.

Medically speaking, through the worlds of bacteria, ("Bja-tur-EA" – or, through the Metaphysical interpretation, the "back door to EA") that encephalization builds up and coerces the hypothalamus – also known as the Little Pyramid in Egypt – and this creates the meningococcal virus (meningitis). It is obtrusive to the light of our higher intelligence. So, if we bring that back into Metaphysics, it is a dance where the ego subjectively ostracizes the emotions concerning who has the priority right to lead.

Have you seen the movie Phenomenon, which starred John

Travolta? That wonderful movie offers a good explanation regarding tumours of the brain, which so many of us receive, when, through our innocence, we do not understand – and this is where we refuse to accept the evolution of the intelligence of the mind. We become trapped in our fear and walk backwards on ourselves, which, of course, gives free rein to allow the tumour its own self-worth.

Through the paths of the ascension process on the quest, we journey back into the cellular structure of our DNA and release the thoughts of the past history of self. That past history is comprised of the life patterns of our parents and grandparents, etc.; through that past history, we become aware of their strengths, as well as their excuses. They are our foundation, and our position is to understand and evolve through and beyond their short-circuits or shortcomings.

Throughout my Shamanic training, I had to learn to be extremely centred on an inner level, watching as I took my thoughts forward into their next step while, simultaneously, my past inheritance pulled me back. I had to experience the worlds of my parents, grandparents, great-grandparents, and many other veils further back as well – all of which were well beyond my own recognition – in order for me to take note of the responsibilities that they had lived up to. I had to make a note of the possibilities of how I could overcome them in order to allow my grandchildren and now my great grandchildren, to be able to experience their own freedom through their inheritance.

During this process, my body changed and warped, my language changed, and my food intake differed from my usual taste. (More about this is explained in my Book IX "Decoding Extra-Terrestrial Intelligence".) My bones (Bja) had to empty out the past fears that I had collected, through me not understanding what I was creating through my thinking. It was a fascinating process to see how I had evolved from my past so that I could become this person I represent today. It took many years of devoted training for me to become totally aware that everything I put into my mouth had to mathematically balance and work with my Alchemy, which automatically adjusted my intelligence as to what I wanted to be able to envisage for myself.

I was learning to understand the process of how we achieve and accomplish the intelligence to enter up into the unconscious mind. To be able to move up into the Divine Intelligence of the Greatest Oracle of the Divine, we have to "cross over the bridge to the other side", as the old saying goes. This is the language of the Shamanic Principles, and it is the last test of treachery that we must exude from our previous third-dimensional existence. The Shaman has to walk through hell to enter into heaven, is the way that the Bible explains it.

The Shaman has to become St John the Divine and earn each page to become the Book of Revelations (to revealing the inner nations). This wonderful last book of the Bible is written in the Divine Intelligence, and it is the third and final initiation of humanity's earnings – and this is where we reach the land of philosophy. I arrived in Germany on St Johannes Day, and I arrived back in Australia ten years later on St Johannes Eve. I thank you, Germany and many other countries across Europe, for your acceptance and the faith that thousands of you earned for yourselves through listening to my words and hearing your own.

I am now explaining to you the reasoning behind the written word at that time, in the land of Egypt. Also, this announcement is in relationship to the Masonic Order of why Hiram Abiff was hit on the back of the head, through holding onto the codes to achieving Solomon's (or the Solo-man's) Temple. Remember, the ego hides under the skirts of the hypothalamus gland, which is the furthest gland towards the back of our head, hence the stories that have been passed down to us of the ego hiding under the garment of God, through its refusal to release its hold over itself!

Egypt is symbolically representing the land we will all become, once our journey is completed; it is victoriously completing the experience of living through the afterlife. (More explanations are in book VII, "Sacred Alphabet and Numerology"). The crossover point is just below the pyramidal system, which is where we enter into the module (notice the change in my vocabulary as I introduce you into the language of Extra-

Terrestrial Intelligence), which is known to us as the medulla oblongata; this area is where our energy enters into other Universes (united verses) for us to become our own spaceship. Now, through the Mayan myths, we can understand the lid of Palenque. (More about this is explained in other books.) We are not hindered from achieving this result, as long as we have the discipline to totally believe in ourselves.

Once we have birthed ourselves through into our Spiritual household, we are entering into the home of our heavenly realms – or what we refer to as the land of the unconscious mind. This section of information is known to us, through the Egyptian philosophies, as the "opening of the mouth ceremony" – which, medically, is referred to as "homunculus", and, through the interpretation of the Latin language, this is referred to as the poor depleted creature, who refuses to change or accept his next step, another reference is the little old man. When we take this word back into the ancient language through the sacred codes, it is explaining to us our relationship to the "heavenly oracle" or the "high monk" who understands life; this is accomplished all through understanding our Soul.

Remember that the word man, through the ancient Sanskrit language, is decoded as "gene", and the plural of this word is men," which is decoded as our "genes". Another reference to the word homunculus, is to the beast within. He is representing both the beast and the devil, and this explanation is where our challenges are presented to us – i.e., as to who is talking to us. This gene, or genetic inheritance, that we are all born with is the largest stumbling block for a human to overcome, through the latter stage of their journey. Is it God or the devil? Do you remember when I introduced you to where the beast likes to hide under the garment of God?

We have now entered up into the Book of Revelations, where we are to face the last of the plagues, as we are introduced up into the sonic sound of our intellectual dictionary or library of the mind. This is represented to us as the worlds of the insect kingdoms, where we use our combustible energy – or mass consciousness – in order to enable us to release our intelligence back to the people. The insect becomes our angelic resonance; look at how some people refer to their inner evaluation of what they think an ET really looks like. It is only through entering into the species of the insect population that our irritations will become deceased, not dis-eased. Once we have found our inner strength, we move beyond the earthly illnesses. It is up here, where the only animal and bird from our past that we attach to ourselves is the mythical species known to us as the gryphon.

Precious students of self-empowerment, I ask that you keep going forward; remember that the sylphs are here to carry you forward, and these are the elementals that Paracelsus spoke about. As a child, my sylphs were the seeds of the dandelion as they left their original plant to find their new resting place. I watched as they were carried by the wind and attracted themselves to me. Also explained brilliantly in the movie Avatar. My grandmother showed me how to make my wish when I needed verification for a question I could not answer. She was shown this energy when she was in China at the turn of the last century, as she was initiated into the esoteric fields of knowledge. Keep sweetening yourself with the nectar that is delivered unto us from God. Negativity will never claim you once you believe that your blood is, as it is in heaven; now head up and move north, and you will open the doorway to live in your eternal home.

It is in this state of mind that you can walk the three worlds as one, –because you are viewing the past, and also the present through the results of accomplishing your own actions, to become your future. Revelations 1:8 explains this to us: "I am Alpha and Omega, the beginning and the ending, saith the Lord, which is and which was and which is to come, the Almighty." This is the home of Greatest Oracle of the Divine, or God.

Have you ever noticed the codes introduced as we enter into the sacred realms of the Vatican? We are symbolically being introduced, unconsciously, to enter up into the unconscious mind; this is presented to us in the Egyptian section, where a statue of a little man stands on the left as you begin to walk through. He is supposedly named Beset or Basset – or, through the Sacred Alphabet, he represents the base of Seth.

He is placed in the section where the two pine cones, which are introduced to us in a Fibonacci sequence, symbolically represent the mathematics of our mind; and these pine cones also symbolically represent the two hemispheres of our brain, and they are situated out on the balcony, overlooking the grounds. Here he is in all his glory! This is the little man who symbolically represents the homunculus, who hides under the garment of God for his own protection.

It is in this area of our brain where the last stand is carried out through the worlds of our fear; it is where we move beyond the emotional blunders that we have used to control ourself as well as others. Our energy then moves up into the hypothalamus gland to be accepted, and then it is brought forward into the pituitary gland, where each thought is measured and balanced before going into the next phase of being rewarded. This is either through being delivered into the left brain, where we must live that experience again – all through our repetitious performance of repeating the same thing over again – or through allowing our thoughts to be placed into the right brain, where the lesson is complete, and the difficulty is erased from our memory banks. In the future, it will not return to interrupt our flow, but it can be used as a reference for others. This bank of information becomes our future Apostolate, where it awaits in our wings to serve us, always.

Through this ascension process, we receive the education to learn and reshape the mind, as we open up and release our DNA. This is the knowledge of our emotions corresponding with one another. My research and studies were through a huge magnifying glass called the third eye, as each cell presented its thoughts to me in an animated form.

The third eye is situated at the top of your nose between your eyes. It brings both eyes into a resonance, where we view everything through the third dimension, and we see everything layer by layer; viewing this through the brain coerces and magnifies our inner sight. The images we see from this eye are reflected up into the forehead. This becomes our inner screen, which is known as "King David" through the stories of the Bible; or "Davidea" or "Davidya" or the inner screen, through the Eastern and Indo-Asian philosophies. The awakening of this inner eye can only happen when we have earned the respect for self to create the opportunity to be in the so-called "waking dream state."

That state of mind explains your dreams to you in picture form while you are asleep. We refer to this area as the "land from where we attain our wisdom", and, in the Shamanic language, we have named it the worlds of "trance-formation". As I have explained previously, this happens when we are in the process of relieving the pressure of our right brain as to how the intelligence of the ego – or left brain – has tried to overrule and suppress it. Once that inner eye is opened, we have the possibility of viewing everything through third-dimensional sight.

Genetically, you have inherited your emotions and ego; your life patterns come from the past. As you begin to understand yourself more clearly, you are given the responsibility to relive and rebirth yourself from those ancient patterns through advancing the self, step by step. This promotes a clearer and more positive future for you to walk towards. In other words, you view and are in attendance to dance with every dis-ease that has collected itself on this planet. If you are positive within yourself, you become an overriding factor of all dis-eases. It is a part of your future inheritance and an introduction into the worlds of Alternative Therapies, Mathematics, Physics or Scientific Understanding.

All the old scholars or prophets had to reach these levels of their own outer boundaries to bring through the information in order for the next generation to evolve into the futuristic hierarchical mind. Through this new understanding, you now have the opportunity to read the Bible correctly, as it has all the answers to teach you how to release the Oracle or the reflections of your Soul! Try and understand it metaphysically, (through the matter of physics) and please learn to look through everything (right–brain) do not just look at it (left-brain). The knowledge and acceptance of this understanding releases the pressure in your cells, allowing your positive thinking to flow more easily throughout you.

Positive thinking allows you to slowly unfold your intelligence, which is embedded in every cell of your body. It lightens the load that you carry and urges you forward, where you begin to take much more interest in yourself and others. Positive thinking returns you to the thinking of your teenage years, where the rebel within becomes alive again. "Go Get'em Girl" became my new motto. You nourish yourself through this thinking, and that opens you up to tread more positively. For the first time in my life, I fell head over heels in love with myself, when I was on that part of my journey. This is the explanation of what we call "Ascension"; to ascend one's self, is to understand and become the collection of our Soul – or the hidden story within us. It is the unfolding of the Myths of the Sages.

Your Notes:

CHAPTER EIGHT

A Cell Is Pure Cosmic Consciousness

A cell builds itself up through the pressure at which its nucleus vibrates, and that vibration is created through the collection of our thinking. When we are in our stillness and listening, our cells collect the energy which is heard by the Higher Self, which becomes weighed and mathematically measured, if hesitation occurs through not digesting the information correctly then that cell becomes entangled and caught up in its self-doubt.

Allow me to pause here and explain our higher self! Another explanation is the "highest of high," by now you understand our higher self once decoded, is that it has been delegated and promoted through earning the position as the "self-governing" one, all through the belief and trust it found in itself, to become the leader. It is in this position where it has the responsibility of looking after those cells that are less fortunate than itself, as it is able to explain through corroboration, which fortifies those thoughts of our thinking back to us. This ultra-surge then opens the next doorway for us to enter. As you can see by these means, the higher- self, gathers its own strength as other cells lose their trepidation (nervousness) as to how they are becoming aware that their inner strength multiplies once they have taken a positive step forward.

If we had somebody on the planet with enough intelligence to know how to remove the pressure from one "dead" cell, we would find that the cell has still retained its life force. Cells become overloaded and choked down with our own negativity, through us not living the thinking that we are busily trying to create. We literally strangle our cells. We are hanging onto a thought that is of no consequence to us when it is repeated. When we can't come to a decision or finish a thought; the difficulty is that the thought then gets locked in. Our cells become blocked; they get choked down through the mind walking backwards, which autonomically hinders our future.

How can the cell function correctly when no life force exists for it to believe in? It can't breathe! It is like pointing a gun to its head with us controlling the trigger. A cell is pure Cosmic Consciousness; thus, it cannot die. The evolution of its own mathematics has created this perfect instrument. It is completeness! So, if it cannot die, we then have the opportunity to know, as our intelligence unfolds, that we can release a new force of life into these same old cells. Now all that information is released through me looking into my own microscope.

We have the opportunity to allow the body to heal itself through the belief and freedom that we can earn through trusting in our highest good, not keeping ourselves hidden through our own fear; it is not forbidden for us to think like this! This is the wonderful mystery of life. This inner dictionary that is co-habitual with our cells has the opportunity to create a new life force, and that substance, which is a higher vibration of Divine Inheritance of self-coagulation, is shaping its own creation through the Alchemy of the mind. Once our thinking has balanced and mirrored back through the illusion of self, our cells are promoted, through their own inference, to replace the old energy with the new.

The thoughts that we create when we are feeling stressed cause the nucleus of the cell to vibrate at a faster speed, and so that cell expands itself with what we call "Universal energy" or "Collective Consciousness". If that energy has nowhere to go, it solidifies itself and becomes a stutter, and then it begins to choke down. The mucus thickens; it builds upon itself and resembles churned butter. This is also the creation of one fat cell; the same thought being returned over and over again.

We overprotect ourselves! In fact, we dry the natural nutrients of the cells up through our stubbornness controlling our thinking. Our body automatically tries to protect itself. It is the energy in motion that collects through this thought, and that, my friends, creates the dis-ease of your future; you never allow yourself to have a positive thought to release it! That is also the beginnings of pimples, which can turn into cysts internally and externally. It all depends on the frequencies emitted through the strength of your thinking as to what you have promoted for it to become.

Before my cancer, I had fifty-two cysts removed from my ovaries: twenty- five off the left ovary and twenty-seven off the right; nobody explained my attitude to me then, so, of course, the cancer was forthcoming. It was only when given the death sentence that I began to take an interest in what and how I was living! I asked myself what my private thoughts had to do with this cancer. From understanding that paragraph of my life, the next step moved itself forward through my own urging. As the years rolled by, someone who had walked my dis-ease before me always crossed my path, and he/she explained a little bit more until my thinking regarding myself, became my priority. That was when my world began to leap ahead.

The vibration of our cells can be positive or negative. Positive, through the happiness of our thoughts understanding themselves; or negative, through our fear stepping into the conversation that we are thinking, and trying to control it. It is the negative that blocks the cell, and the positive that releases and heals. Stress is a strong vibration, and a vibration is the relationship to the inner light; it is a harmonic vibration that interferes to an outer urgency. It is a positive reaction in our own innocence of trying to achieve and accomplish the light. The only way to relieve stress in our body is to allow that harmonic convergence within us to be in tune with itself.

For example, having the same thought about a difficult situation, over and over again, and staying in that stressful thinking repeatedly, causes the mucus to gel, and this then sets the scene for the churned-butter effect. That blockage, over time, creates the relationship to form a dis-ease. We give a title to this form through the codes of consciousness, and then we have a name for what we are creating. Giving something a name appeases the stress factor, says the ego. If we don't have a name for it, we panic. The thought is not consciously or subconsciously aware of this dis-ease; it is all stored in the unconscious mind, our own memory banks, and this is the evolution of our Soul releasing itself. Pay attention when the first pain begins.

A dis-ease is a formation of coded mathematics reclining into a disposition of safety. Our thoughts are measured through their own circumference, according to the force of the vibration we place in our thinking. The emotion called "hate" – and I like to refer to hate as an extreme lack of loyalty in one's self – is the strongest of measures. This thought, if pressurized over a long period, creates cancer. Cancer cannot be created or activated without that emotion being forced into its life by our thinking! This is a coded language of Collective Behaviour, and the measurement of each cell nurtures the life force of that dis-ease.

Your Notes:

CHAPTER NINE

The HIV/AIDS Virus

Allow me to move on and explain the HIV/AIDS virus to you in a Metaphysical way, again through my research of my own collective experiences. We are aware metaphysically that the rampant HIV/AIDS begins its journey with the hatred of the father within. I accepted that; when my patients began coming for healing, I had the opportunity to question that explanation. Slowly, over time, with many hundreds of AIDS patients coming, through their permission to heal through regressional therapy, I could bring the mosaics of the dis-ease together and build up my own understanding of the story.

It can symbolically represent the father figure through this man's childhood, which sets the scene into reaching its own zenith. It is a force of one thought that builds itself up into its next hierarchical mind. This then becomes hatred of the father within, who is symbolically representing your Higher Self. Can you see here, as in the previous story, what pressure we are doing to the central nervous system? It affects the endocrine system (child), immune system (teenager), and lymphatic system (matriarch). You then go on to detest your own future, and this builds up and registers with the unconscious. As this thought grows into its own compatibility, it then reaches up into the lymphatic system, wanting to reach its own zenith, and the Overlord has to step in. There is no longer any respect for self. It is the primal sexual attitude, protecting itself from the spiritual emotional knowledge. It is the fear of stepping up to one's own self-acclaim. Where cancer is created through the hatred of self and others, AIDS is an advanced stage through the misrepresentation of the God within.

This is where some people that have inherited the dis-ease have turned to face the same sex! Please allow me to explain the dis-ease through the Metaphysical language to begin with. Through the Laws of the Universe, when we turn to a relationship of same sex, we mutate our self into a false acclaim. We are trying to balance and create a law that we find applicable unto our self; remember this word "unto" is delivered from above, down to our self. This excuse that we make is to free us of the responsibility of nurturing our self, back into our own Divine Inheritance. We collapse back into our own attitude, which gives our ego comfort and protection.

How does a government create a law that gives this excuse its own life force? How can the Collective Consciousness add up its own mathematics? It only creates more Karma for the whole of humanity to digest. This may not affect the AIDS patients personally. And yet, it will affect humanity as a whole! Where are we heading to promote the future for the next generation? I am explaining the energy of the Collective Consciousness – and how this energy must realize its own growth for us to inherit – so that we can all continue on. The more excuses we search for, the greater the responsibilities that we are placing on to the next generation's shoulders, as well as the rest of society.

Most of my patients were beautiful young men who came to me of their own free will, through one of my first patients explaining to his friends that through understanding how the dis-ease collected itself, he could understand himself for the first time in his life. He realized that he had been given a choice of endowment. I stopped counting when the number of patients got into the hundreds. Through Regressional Therapy seminars, those patients had the opportunity to relive their earlier worlds of emotion, which they had deliberately blocked and tucked away. This old attitude had kept them safe and out of harm's way – or so they thought.

It was through their anger conforming to tears – through allowing themselves to open up into their emotional mind – that they could rebalance their understanding of what they had allowed themselves to believe was their truth. Tears are a baptism that anoints our ego. They found that they had hidden underneath their own higher garments – and behind the attitude of their mother figure – which means that they had been innocently searching for security from their upheaval to protect their own emotional mind. Their mother's garment allowed them to create a veil that would support and hide them even more.

For two men to come together, one of them must change his ideals and become the feminine principle. There can only be one winner in a relationship, and that is the strongest one. This is part of the Laws of the Universe. The same is true in lesbian relationships, only the roles are reversed; they choose to hide behind the father figure, which allows them also to create a veil to support their inner nourishment.

The changes were noticeable when I explained different ideas for them to formulate about their many personalities – which were all trying to vie for the top position of controlling the others – as to how they could learn to relax their minds; it slowly led them into earning a meditation of accepting their own free will, and this presented to them the opportunity to look through their emotional bodies from an inner level. Their minds learned to understand and accept the growth of their own intelligence, and their inner strength became their power as it collected into its own conformity. You see, the little boy had to grow up and become a man. He could no longer accept his old illusions. The women I counselled had to accept and release the hidden woman within. Throughout its creation, the dis-ease registered the truth that they did not want to look at, and refused to understand, back to them. It did not matter what age they were; in reality, it has to do with the attitude of their mind; they had nourished themselves from their own expectations.

As those young people slowly went into remission, their attitude picked up, as they had altered their native within; through their acceptance of self, they began to contribute more importance, to their thinking. For the first time in a long time, they could believe in themselves and had the pleasure of rearranging their thoughts. Their judgment of self, had reached its zenith, and they could then learn to love and accept who they truly were. We each have the choice to choose our own future, and I loved them for their honesty of who they were, are, and will become.

So now we can accept this information regarding the Metaphysical understanding through the language of the Divine Inheritance. Each tribe collects and follows the rules that have mathematically collected on their behalf. We all belong to the Collective, as we are all equal through the eyes of God or these Universal Laws. Both are one and the same. There is no Judgment that is delivered to us from above, only Justice. The legal proceedings begin with you.

When the first female heterosexual patient with AIDS came to me, I had to balance my justice of all the previous connotations that I had. The woman was an executive in a large male-dominated company. She had not had a sexual relationship for twelve years. She had programmed that life over a number of years so that she could empower herself up into her career. So how did she contract the dis-ease?

Back to the drawing board I went and offered her Regressional Therapy. She was hesitant to succumb to this; she just wanted to hear my story. She kept on returning for another appointment, and, over the next few weeks, I kept on talking and explaining to her the journey of our thinking, and how it creates a positive attitude to the self. She was so angry with me, at first, for reminding her of her past. Over time, I felt her strength begin to change;

I watched as the woman within began to return home, back inside herself. She slowly walked back into her past thoughts; finally, at her suggestion, we began the Regressional Therapy.

Back we went into her yesterdays, and there it was. She was an only child. Throughout her life, her father had kept on reminding her that he had wanted a boy child, not a girl. After all, how could a female carry his name forward? Her mother had never had a thought of her own; she did as she was told, so no welcome had come for this girl into that family. She could not find the strength to become her own voice through her father and his overpowering attitude.

So, over the years, the male role came into being, and the woman hid behind her skirts – or the layers of her emotional mind that she had produced for her own protection. Her masculine attitude had to reign supreme, as she was determined that it had to get her to where she had to go! She was bastardizing herself, so, of course, the HIV/AIDS energy found a home.

After many months of explaining the role, she had created for herself, and her acceptance of understanding this dis-ease, she went into remission over the next twelve months; in the ensuing years, she began a new relationship. Her first child, who was born when she was in her early forties, was free of the dis-ease. So, it is not all doom and gloom. If the correct education is applied to your mind, and you can see the results through understanding your intelligence, then this dis-ease has the opportunity to correct its own flow of life!

At this point in time of reaching an ending of this millennium, we understand that every six seconds, HIV/AIDS conquers one more human. These seconds are diminishing very quickly. The largest most-populated countries – that also have the same Divine Inheritance – automatically fit the bill at this time.

What is interesting about this dis-ease is that it is consuming more women than men in third world countries. Why? One word: sacrifice! Their value of self-worth is insurmountable, and they have no say in the sexual act. Those women, through their sacrifice to men, receive the HIV/AIDS virus through their own sacrifice to themselves. Forgive them father for they know not what they do! The men who rape those women are raping their own intelligence, or their own emotional mind, through the frustration of not understanding their own Divinity, and they are attacking their own God within.

Allow me to go further regarding the heavily populated countries with a high count of HIV/AIDS cases. As our responsibility to self-gathers and accumulates, we can adjust their standard of education. We have the possibilities of showing them how they can learn to help themselves; through educating them, we will see a difference in the statistics of the dis-ease, and medication will change and become much more affordable for all. We will be held responsible for our own worthiness, and this comes from our action through creating our self-will. This will of ours has to settle its responsibilities with the Divine will of the universal law. I am speaking to you from the right brain now, not the left!

The responsibility, in the first place, begins with us, and those less fortunate have the opportunity to follow on. That is how I explained the story to those young men who had AIDS; I had a responsibility to explain to them through my learning and earning of my own education.

At the last HIV/AIDS conference, I noted that there was mention of trying to admit to the responsibility of not participating in the sexual act. Wow!! Of course, that is right! Although, to begin with, we have to understand that these urges are our excuses of not accepting our own self-worth. Gently and firmly, we must reflect the truth back to humanity, and we are hoping that they will begin to listen and accept their next positive thought. Viruses will keep on manifesting to show us the way until we get it right. Just like our last virus we have named COVID-19. Millions of people have passed over (died), all from one virus. We have certainly reaped what we have sewn.

All of those wonderful people with AIDS, which is still an ongoing performance, are living up to the expectations of their own DNA. Through the frustration of their own thinking, they will, in time, begin to change their attitude as their own self-worth evolves. People are receiving the AIDS virus as an example to the planet of what we still have to overcome through the thoughts of our Collective Mind (Consciousness). My hope is that my grandchildren and their grandchildren have the pleasure of seeing their world as I do.

One person every six seconds receives the HIV/AIDS virus. Mathematically, that is 10 per minute, 600 per hour, and 14,400 people per day. This code is similar to the numbers written in the Book of Revelations, and it is also carved on the forehead of King "Tut-Ankh-Amun"; there is only one less zero! It is a code of the inheritance from the Divine Intelligence! We are on the way to reaching a zenith; so, what are we portending to happen next? And here it is, for the last three years it has been COVID-19.

Those larger countries represent millions of people who live in symbolic conditions, and who have difficulties in coercing with understanding the laws of the Collective. They are listening, but they have great difficulty in hearing their own self-worth. There are billions of people who are living in poverty conditions through self-denial. Is this how the "Greatest Oracle of the Divine" wants them to live, or is this how these "Universal Laws" reflect and release back to us what we are doing through our innocence of not living up to our own higher intelligence? Remember that yearning is the sexual flow, learning is the acceptance and education, and earning, the last of the three, is the action that is positively created through all three coming together.

When is the world going to realize that pregnancy is an excuse for this current generation? It is not through inhibiting the next! We can see which one of these has taken priority when the HIV/AIDS count has climbed beyond the freedom of recognizing the wisdom of ourselves. Is this showing us the future inheritance of our intelligence?

Do you see how these cosmic laws reimburse back to us, our inner harmony or anointed favours through creating pregnancy? Why does a woman have to prostitute herself to herself? When can she begin to understand and accept her truth regarding the freedom of self? We can now understand why little children must accept their mother's overture; they 'shepherd their mother's innocence' – or is it ignorance? – is the nicest way that I can explain this to you.

The countries that are overpopulated must begin to look at their own future, and, more importantly, their lack of education, which can only manifest through the lack of security within; our attitude stands to attention from our intelligence realizing itself. Wisdom begins to release through the acceptance of our own understanding and the belief we attain in the Collective Inheritance; in other words, these are our future expectations.

Let us discuss the world's population for a moment. This is a planet where the majority understands the three dimensions of thought, and, through understanding ourselves more thoroughly, we are on the way up to discovering and inheriting the fourth dimension. We have three classes to tune into, beginning with the lower, then up to the middle, and up further into the higher mind. Does the lower have to yearn and deplete itself for the middle, or does the middle have to learn and deplete itself for the higher, in order to earn and accept its own inheritance? Yes, that is the gift that we have earned for ourselves! When we do move forward, our mirror must then be reversed back down the line. The higher we ascend, the more responsible we become – for all of humanity to view. We become their light, their silence, and their wisdom.

Your Notes:

CHAPTER TEN

The Mind Of The Pedophile

Allow me to bring a few extra paragraphs to your attention in order to explain the energy of the mind of a pedophile. Here we see similarities of the same story. The mind of the pedophile is a much deeper bastardization of self, and it attacks the innocence of the child, whereby the pedophile rapes the child of their own self-worth. The child is the innocent emotional mind, which must have the opportunity to learn to accept its own responsibility in order to grow and foster itself. The pedophile reflects back through society its own molestation of what he/she is doing to their inner self – that is, the promise of their next thought. We also refer to the next thought as the "child within", so, for God's sake, teach it to have faith to believe in itself.

The pedophile's mind is raping itself through the discomfort of their own Soul reflecting their own emotional values back to themself. The illusion that the pedophile has earned regarding him/herself mirrors back to themself the results of their individual thinking, which is stored in the aura. This happens through the deprivation of self, which collects and builds itself up through the concordance of all – or from the God within who is surmounting its own responsibilities.

Through the pedophile's own inheritance – and this is the culmination of the life that they are living in the moment – the ego urges each individual to destroy the self. The unconscious mind – or God within – takes over and directs the flow of the pedophile's own justice. When the pedophile fears for themself, the natural primal urge is to attack those who cannot defend themselves. It is the pedophile's own sexual energy – which they have locked in through masturbating with their own mind – that creates the hatred which manifests and takes control. The pedophile attacks the innocent, through that child becoming a mirror of what the pedophile's wisdom is showing them of their own future.

When children are brought into an incestuous relationship, the majority of them do not speak of this contact to their mother, each knowing that she does not want to know or listen. Why? She is also trapped into this same mould of excusable self. Remember that, when we listen to someone else, it is first brought through to the left brain. "Listening" to a story is paying attention to and looking at the difficulty. "Hearing" the same story is a different vibration; "to hear" means to bring the information inside one's self, this occurs through the right hemisphere of our brain, where we are given the opportunity to look through the situation; in other words, we are much more aware of knowing right from wrong. Therefore, which one assists us to realize our truth – listening or hearing, or, which one gives us the opportunity to stabilize our mind?

Allow me to explain this story further. Through the collection of the sacred path, it is a mathematical creation of a 40-degree circle – or void – which is created through the aura that is brought into its own intuition or institution. This cohabitates in the mass of our own consciousness, entering into the mastoid area through the right ear and up into the right brain. Our mastoids receive accordingly through the balancing of the inner ear, and this directs the flow of adjustment.

If we have difficulties with our left ear, it is because we are refusing to accept our own truth. We are afraid to hear the truth that is released to us through our own Divinity. To ease the pressure for you about this word, Divinity is a collective of how we eclectically arc into accepting our responsibility. Therefore, we choose to listen and not to hear. When we have the same problem as our children, we refrain from understanding the equation; we choose to turn a deaf ear to the subject. Maybe now you can understand the child who is born deaf.

I realize that all this information is extremely strenuous for you to process; please put the book down and take a glass of water to refresh your mind, as this allows my words to filter through your cells. A special thank-you for continuing to read the story so far!
Your Notes:

CHAPTER ELEVEN

Our Responsibilities

Let us all move on to another difficulty that we must learn to overcome. If we are indentured through our intelligence opening up into the higher realms, we have an added responsibility to assist with an underdeveloped country. The statistics (statistics from around 2006) are alerting us to the fact that one child dies every five seconds as a result of having no food to eat. These statistics are informing us that 17,280 children die from starvation every day – that is, in each 24-hour period. A point to remember regarding the innocence of these children is that starvation kills a much greater percentage of people than the AIDS virus does. These children, supposedly, are the future inheritance of this planet! So, we have 14,400 people each day succumbing to the AIDS virus, and, when we add these two figures together, we have a total of 31,680 deaths per day – not counting the other illnesses that we are also busily creating.

War is a causal point with me; in regard to my own emotional self, I have never believed in war, yet I fell in love with a soldier. Our eyes met across the table, and his eyes sparkled in recognition of my emotional upheaval at that time. He had just joined the army and still had years of service to give. We married two years later, and, throughout our relationship, the army ruled over our lives. He had made a commitment, and he very quickly climbed up the ladder to earn his stripes. I was so very proud when he was in his uniform and on parade. His looks made my heart sing.

He brought changes to the way I had been brought up. He became a marksman with many different guns and ammunition, where he held these implements in the highest regard – reverence, really. Most of my immediate family were conscientious objectors who would not take up a gun. They never walked away from what humanity had created, and they played their part in the game, always there in the front lines as stretcher-bearers and first-aid workers. Their photos proudly hang in the war museums of my country, alongside those who held the guns in their hands.

The women of my family tribe worked beside their men twenty-four hours a day – and when the men went away to war, it was left up to the women to the planting of grain, shearing the sheep, and milking the cows in order to supply our country's soldiers with their food and uniforms. The grain had to be harvested at the right time so that it was free of rust, and the sheep had to be raised to perfection so that their meat could be cooked properly – and all this was for the soldiers' food. The fleece was kept clean so that it could be spun into wool for the soldiers' uniforms. The cows had to be milked twice a day. Plus, the other daily chores – butter to churn, cheese to make, beef to be supplied. Our complete household belonged to feeding the men at war. However, this did not mean that we had to follow the mainstream thought. We knew, through our understanding of why we were here – which was to obtain a benefit for mankind – that our purpose was not to be to the detriment of others being deprived of their life at an early age. And, more importantly, we believed that those men who were injured also had the chance to receive the blessing for the commitment that they had made.

The elder women of our family tribe cooked for the household and looked after the little ones, while the young mothers were out in the paddocks and fields. In the evenings, the women knitted socks from our wool, which was spun into yarn to keep the soldiers' feet warm. So, you see, I have been shown both sides of the reasoning behind the word war. It was interesting to note that on this journey, through me opening up into the mathematical codes of each word, I could explain what each letter represented in a positive outcome and that through this word War, I was informed that our Wisdom Ascends and Releases.

Thus, it came as quite a shock to me when I finally understood the language of the codes of the Bible – i.e., that the written word never explained how to kill one another. My tribe was right! Let us look at the correct way to view this word kill through the Collective Consciousness: "through my Knowledge, my Intelligence is the relationship to my Life". The word has two ll s. So this leads us to believe that "to kill" means that our knowledge – or our knowing is ill. Now allow me to introduce you to another word that sounds familiar: keel. In the ancient language, the word kill did not exist, because the earlier alphabet did not have the letter i. So now we view the word keel through another window; the dictionary describes this word as meaning "a timber or steel structure along the base of the ship". However, when someone "keels over", it means that he/she collapses. Is it through our own momentum being out of balance that we overturn?

Please remember that it was through the way in which each word was pronounced – that is, how it was heard from one person to the other – that each sound was carried forward into the Collective. If these codes that my teachers taught to me are to be believed, it means that what I have always believed in is true. We have yet to understand the Universal language and teachings as to the evolution of how these stories have been collected and placed in the Bible. It is through the innocence of our own understanding of the past, that our thoughts relate to how we have understood the original stories written in the Bible.

Let the Divine Intelligence remind you, as stated in Genesis 9:6, "Whoso sheddeth man's blood, by man shall his blood be shed: for in the image of God made he man." Our blatant desire always looks for "substantial" control to substitute for the easy way out! As previously stated, through the codes, the word war is interpreted as "wisdom ascending and releasing". The explanation through the "Schools of Secrets" are the teachings that all war is a war of self; this war of self- fights for its own supremacy, through our ego trying to over-control our emotions – it is not really about fighting with one another.

Now that I have accomplished my earthly life and am now travelling around the planet explaining the next step of our emotional intelligence, I have listened to and shared tears with hundreds of men – some who fought against my country, and others who stood side by side with us. All of them regret the tormented mind that they have endured for most of their lives. When they revisit their memory banks as their thoughts bring these memories back to their attention, they find that these memories are still wrapped around them, and they know that their guilt still reigns supreme. They were young men at the time of these wars, and they lost brothers, other family, and friends; many of them feel that they deprived those sacrificial men of their own life.

War is a lesson for you to understand the Universal Law of your own personal inheritance, and this goes for every region that we see in front of our eyes in this place that we call home. When speaking of war, every myth and every story of the Bible is explaining a hidden language through the Metaphysical resonance; and, so far, we are still on level 1 regarding how we have understood the sacred numerical codes. We will make huge changes throughout the Collective when we return our thinking back into ourselves before we speak and release our thoughts to others.

This is the balanced relationship regarding our sense of reality, which we release and must live by from the deliverance of the unconscious mind. How many men have died to bring peace to the world? Millions and millions and millions, and so on. Take a peek at your TV screen, and show me a news service that is free from war. Enough said! When we hesitate to know and understand ourselves, negativity has free rein to rise up and override our positivity. That's life! When we do not understand ourselves, we search for a safety harness of comfort from others, as we cannot find it within ourself, and, by doing so, we allow our ego to reign supreme. Do you see how we could eradicate every dis-ease or war on the planet, when we understand this paragraph?

Over the millennia, we have assumed the explanations of the carving on the walls, thinking that our expectations can only be conquered through defiling others – when, all the time, the message was for you, the individual human, to understand how you can bring your thoughts into balance with one another. These images, especially in Egypt, are not explaining a war between nations; rather, they are alerting us to the facts of the inner consequences that we create for ourselves when we fear the in-known. Those chariots with rearing horses are not describing a war with other nations; they are explaining a war between your personalities, which are struggling for their own right to reign supreme through becoming their own Spiritual strength.

We now understand that HIV/AIDS is created through our sexual thoughts overpowering our emotions. For, sex is a form of control that we allow to have free rein innocently over ourself, when the ego is confined through an eclectic invasion. Remember that this is a religious (through the Latin interpretation, is explaining to us, that we are linking back to our source) experience that we are tuned into through the teachings of our ultimate gathering of our unconscious mind. The ego has to look for an excuse – or comfort – in order to release. It is like representing a church. It sounds confusing, doesn't it? The word church can be decoded as follows: (CH) "energy", (UR) "understanding and releasing", (CH) "energy". Now, that is quite a different explanation! The outer perspective of our thinking, is hidden within, where our ego is afraid to trust that which it refuses to know. Therefore, through our ego we disregard that knowing or coded language, that we are implanted with, before our birth.

Your Notes:

CHAPTER TWELVE

Disease, Cancer And The Thyroid

Let us take a peek into another subject that is also of a nonconformist nature. The ratio of men to women on this planet is 8 to 1. Why? As a result of the 90-day pregestational period, through the mathematical accruing of the mother's storehouse of thoughts; in other words, she had to come to a decision about where, or in what direction, her thoughts were building up to create for her, and she could not find the courage within herself to do a thing about it. She placed her thoughts in the "too-hard basket" and hid it behind the door. So, through the Collective, this new species of humanity had to be born male; she could not find the power within herself to live up to, or recognize her own thoughts.

Through her own unhappiness, she was forcibly trapped in her emotional mind and could not get out; as a result, pregnancy had to follow. This is the Divine will of God. The Soul is neither male nor female; it is the mathematical sum of the wholeness. The deliverance of whether you have a male or female child is totally dependent on the mathematics of what is lacking in your thinking at that time.

Can you begin to understand how the dis-ease HIV/AIDS is now affecting more women than men? Man has not yet earned, and, through the detriment of his own mind, he has overpowered woman; and, woman, through her sacrificing herself, has now been overtaken by the male species. Thus, the battle begins, and we watch the collapse within both male and female as they step forward to create another futuristic dis-ease.

We know that dis-ease can only manifest in a cell through the fear that is still trapped within our self. We condense that cell through our refusal of accepting our consciousness; it is not through consciousness expanding itself. Remember that the greatest fear of humanity is the fear of stepping in to understand the self. The dis-ease, or blockage, in the cell is a negative impulse that creates its own life force within the body. If we can now understand and accept how that cell created its own blockage, nothing exists that we cannot heal within ourselves. When a cell is blocked off by a thought – and it is a strong-enough thought – it becomes an enemy to itself in its own right, and it searches for support and must feed itself off other cells, usually of same mind!

For example, when one cancerous cell exists in the body – and the hatred that you have already created through your thinking is strong enough – that thought triggers the cell into action. All the other cells around it, sacrifice themselves to the power of that one cell, owing to its strength, and its power consumes them. (Is this not how war is created?) Thus, the strength of just one of your thoughts – and how long you harbor and hide that thought – is what determines the strength with which the dis-ease will manifest; therefore, you have opened the doorway as to what the dis-ease must become. In other words, you have relied on that negative thought, as it has created a zone of comfort for your ego, where your excuses have always been supported.

The cell that is chosen to measure that dis-ease is through the principles of the unconscious mind's decision, searching through you, for a relationship of compatibility. When a dis-ease is in the making, it travels – or traverses – along your inner dictionary, which is your central nervous system, searching for the weakest part of the body.

Its compatibility is through the relationship of the energy that must be equalized through the detriment of your thinking. Through your attitude, you inherit the dis-ease that it is your right to claim. The infected cell is the right one to collaborate with the unconscious mind, and it takes responsibility for the dis-ease to manifest into its own life force.

Every human has cancer and leukemia cells – along with every other dis- ease known to man – and those cells are energies that the Collective Consciousness has inherited on our behalf. All that is in the Collective of our consciousness, is available to all of us, and we receive the benefit of it all. Our inherent dis-ease is constructed through the emotional instability that we apply to ourselves.

If our thinking measures with the dis-ease stored in the Collective, the mathematics of the Collective Consciousness must force it to find its home base. We call this an "electromagnetic field". Energy attracts attention! Nobody in our educational systems has yet explained to us that, as we think a negative thought, we must understand and accept it in order to earn the ability to release it!

The dis-ease created in those cells cannot progress when we have understood and accepted the reason why we attracted and connected with it in the first place. Okay, that may sound a bit awkward, so let me explain it again, backwards. Once we attract a dis-ease to ourselves, we then must learn how to accept this sentence (punishment decided by a higher Court of Law) that we have been given, therefore, we must learn how to change this word into sentience (where we are capable of feeling things differently, which autonomically applicates changes to our thinking) and, through that acceptance, we begin to understand the dis-ease. This understanding then halts us in our thinking, and so we prepare to change our way of life.

As we take on this new responsibility, the energy from the dis-ease begins to falter. Its life force becomes starved of its own oxygen – or energy – and so, first, it must relinquish its life force, and then, it must surrender to the higher source within. The lymphatic system – the Overlord – then has the chance to rebalance our thinking. Symbolically, this finite web is God's hand touching us. We have to come back into the gestation of the planet; we have to learn to come through our heart, as it is the pump station to every facet of our being, not step over it, and, more importantly, not take a wide berth around it. This is the only way for the future generations to have the possibility to inherit the program of what we have forwarded on to them.

Over the years, I have given many lectures to cancer groups, explaining to them how they can prepare their mind to release this energy that has attacked their cells so grievously. My meditations are strong and forceful, not soft and pliable, as I found that most people must have an inner strength that is able to lift them up and out of the bondage in which the cancer has tried to envelop them. I ask them to go into their body, seat themselves inside the cancer, and meet the dis-ease head on. Many have gone up into their own Divinity, and, through their newly found belief, they have placed themselves into a form of remission. We don't stop there; we go on fortifying our strength until our inner light switches on and we receive the "all clear".

We attract the dis-eases that are equivalent and relevant to our thinking. For example, the person who has a blockage in their thyroid is refusing to speak their inner truth, through the coercion of the ego not wanting to comply with its own justice, which we now know is the left hemisphere of the brain controlling their ultimate thinking. If this had affected the parathyroid, it would relate to the right hemisphere of the brain being held up through this previous power. So, the dilemma grows up and multiplies itself. The positive self was in the wings, waiting to come through, but that person refused to acknowledge and accept their own higher realm of intellect.

This is the explanation of the thyroid through the biblical hierarchy: The thyroid is the microphone to our God within; it is also known as the Archangel, Lord Michael. Through the Arabic principles, it is called the "Drach-ab-Bja", the "dragon's breath". This explains why we cough.

A cough creates itself through a congestion of blocked energy, and, if we keep on ignoring it and don't pay attention, it becomes bronchitis, which sets the stage for pneumonia and opens the doorway to many other diseases. The dis-ease adds up its own mathematics to become more pronounced, as it has been given the choice to travel whatever pathway it designs for itself.

Do you see how that one thought begins to consume all of your energy? No excuses, please! Remember that everything that happens to us is a directive from our unconscious mind. The ego is still demanding control of our intelligence.

If you have something to say, please take a deeper breath, speak out your thoughts, and release your pent-up thinking.

You will soon realize what you have spoken to yourself and others, when you or they become offended. If you don't want to speak it out to others, go tell it to a tree. The tree will just stand there and listen to you; it will not run away, and that is why we call it a "stand" of trees. The point is this: For God's sake – get those words out!

Cancer of the throat is in its eminence. When you think of the word thyroid, (Thy-roid is the old word for rod, please remember these words of the 23rd Psalm: "Thy rod and thy staff, they comfort me all the days of my life, and I will dwell in the house of the Lord forever." The message pertaining to this verse into the metaphysical interpretation is informing us that once we understand and are reliant upon ourself, our believe in ourself has placed us up into the land of freedom. When we close that microphone down, through our own hesitation to speak out what we want to say, the next positive thought calls out: "I wish to speak!" But we're not listening to that thought, either! If that thought cannot be released, it reverses its psyche and becomes blocked, which allows the ego to again attack the emotional right brain.

Remember the next positive thought is also symbolically referred to as the "child within", and this is connected to the symbolic story of Mary with the baby Jesus. This symbolic figure has been returned to us over and over again as a premonition, which is a reminder for the emotional mind to prepare for the birth of our next thought, which, in turn, is an inner message for the ego to be able to release on an outer constituency.

Dis-ease is created by working against the thoughts that you feel are necessary for you to hold onto. In other words, the importance of the word dis-ease is a repetition of how you are totally bent on destroying yourself! Stop nourishing it! You must not mother, father, protect, or make excuses for it. That only feeds it; which allows it to create more strength to foster itself.

Learn the art of meditation, it is amazing what you will learn in regards to yourself! The quietening of your mind will place you into a realm you have not walked into before. Take your time and learn to listen to your silence. This may take a while in the beginning so please persevere with allowing this silence to spread its way throughout your body. Over time, you will notice the difference in your thinking, your planning, your preparation, your gathering of new ideas, your relaxed mind, I could go on and on here. Just do it!

Your Notes:

CHAPTER THIRTEEN

Intellectual Disability

Let us now move on into the worlds of intellectual disability. This is a space of training that took me a number of years to see through the eyes of the Metaphysical resonance; it became so much more involved as I stepped up each rung of my internal ladder. This dis-ease affects a tremendous percentage of humanity, whether we are aware of it or not! I had to research each stage from the beginning until I could read the previous generation's thoughts as to how they refused to add to the responsibility of the contentment that they had wished for themselves. Sometimes I was lucky enough to have three generations of the one family present, and then much to my surprise, I found that I was receiving the same story in instalments.

We now understand, through the codes, that the word ill equates to; the "intellectual relationship to life". It begins with an excuse of self, which then triggers the bacterium to enter into the doorways of the ventricles of the heart, which are then triggered up through the neural pathways to enter up into the brain. It is the introduction to the Divine experience of understanding the unconscious mind. I feel that this has a lot to do with the cohabitation of the meninges, which are those three magical membranes that envelop the brain and spinal cord. Through our piousness (pia mater) of self, we weave our thoughts together through the arachnoid, which collects and sustains our durability (dura mater). The difficulty is that these individuals are forced unconsciously, through their previous generations, to turn their back on their own intelligence.

Meeting and communicating with intellectually disabled people on an esoteric level was a totally new experience for me. They spoke the language of a hidden world, through the language of their body movement, which took me seven long years to bring the codes together. They have placed so many veils around the fears that are trapped within – feeling that no one will notice them – that they have pushed themselves even further into the background emotionally, through the outlandish behaviour of their ego having free rein. And the ego's free rein is the direct result of their thoughts being forced to sacrifice themselves through their previous inheritance.

A child who is born with an intellectual disability is a follow-through of the Soul energy – or that family's DNA. In most cases, if we meandered back through 200 years of that family's history, we would see the same case presenting itself down through that lineage. It must return back through the family tribe until it is understood by the Elders of their own personal tribal law– all through their success in understanding their own inheritance. These adjustments can then be cleared in order for that tribe to inherit a positive future.

Please bear with me as I try to explain the world of these intellectually disabled children and adults to you. I could understand them perfectly. Initially, I watched their body language through the movements of their arms and legs and then picked up the language of their fingers, which is explaining their final analysis of their combined mind. Each movement of their body represented an emotional response to the level of the intelligence of their inner language. By moving their shoulder, raising an arm, or crossing their legs, their unconscious mind delivered an autonomic response to me and I had to be aware of its findings.

Through the Indo-Asian influences, we announce them as the language of the Mudras. Throughout my personal journey to understand the Shamanic resonance, I found that my fingers began to communicate back to me on a telepathic level – that is, they were talking back to me. My teachers referred to this agreement between "me, myself, and I" as the language of the stars. It was as if my whole body had begun to produce my own music to orchestrate the thoughts in my mind as I learned to release my inner silence. I learned to allow my fingers to produce my next thought, and I learned very quickly to follow their influences, as they seemed to have much more wisdom than I did – and they knew more than I did, too. The Arabic influences also announce this hidden language, and we can see this as we link our mind into the postures carved or painted on the walls. We of the Western influences are only now beginning to be introduced to this form of telepathic inheritance. Once we have accepted and returned our intelligence back to ourselves, we can all learn that silent body language.

I also watched which way they twisted their bodies and created their facial expressions. When they rubbed their eyes, I noticed whether it was above or below the eye. I had to take note of the first contact with their skin as they began to express their inner sentences; where their fingers touched their ears; how they moved around the nose area – the messages went on and on, year after year. The messages were coming from the reflection of their Soul; another explanation is that the messages came through the Oracle releasing itself from within – all of which are the autonomic responses working on our behalf. I took particular notice of how their unconscious mind telepathically spoke to me through this system reflecting the difficulties that the person was living under. I realized, as it first began, that this was to allay the fear in me so that I would carry through being non-judgmental to their behaviour.

As I slowly came to understand their intelligence, I found that I was becoming more aware of this hidden language, which is heralded on to us, through the power of telepathic communication. It could not lie to me, as it was delivered through their Divine principles. These people are on their own inner quest, and they have been trapped through a lack of explanation from anyone regarding their illness. No one could inform or explain to them why they had to inherit their dis-ease. We cannot keep on using God as an excuse! "It is God's plan!" I have heard that more than a thousand times. Well, if we are all made in the likeness of God, can someone please explain to me why we keep on using him as our own excuse? Let me repeat: These wonderful people have had no one to help them understand the reasons of why they have had to inherit this dis-ease. People are trained to reply to the difficulties of these people, yet no one can explain to them that they have the opportunity to eradicate this mentality out of the family lineage. Well, I can explain it!

It begins through a world of loneliness – way back in the

past grandmother's time – when, through her loneliness, she created a detachment of self. She had no one to listen to her and no one to share her inner thoughts with, mainly due to an overbearing partner or parent who constantly belittled her, which became a thorn – or, to use a better word, sword – in her side. She found solace in her unconscious mind, which helped prepare the future generations of that family for the battle ahead, as they felt safe and protected in that space. We are all aware that the unconscious mind is the House of God or the complete 'Temple of Records.' As a result, the silent space had built up and collected its strength over the following generations, and this was autonomically passed down through their tribal system, genetically, so it became more inherent in the future. On a conscious level, humanity is unaware of everyone else's thoughts; thus, each person only protects themselves, which allows them to use others as an excuse. This opens a doorway of decline, where we slide down our scale and are automatically drawn into judging others. If only they could have been so busy trying to understand their own intelligence! The superiority of the left brain is showing us, once again, how it wants to stay in control, which inhibits our overall growth.

If we look at a child with Down's syndrome, we can understand more clearly the role that this child must assume. Birthing a child who has inherited this dis-ease usually occurs when a woman is around middle age. Why? The mother is accepting a pregnancy that she is no longer waiting for, and she is past excusing herself for her own intelligence. The higher the intelligence of the mother, the more she becomes bruised through her ego overpowering her; and, through this event, she sets the patterns of the child's building frame. If a younger woman births the child, it is through her overreacting to her own parental overture. She has, through her intellect, become her own parent, and she feels that it is no longer applicable for her to have a need to create a pregnancy.

Yes, every child can be helped if only we understood more of this amazing inner hidden language. The same story goes for any child born with a dis-ease – the child must inherit the mother's false acclaim through her lack of respect for herself – and I explain these consequences with the greatest respect for all of you. If I could go through all of these experiences to learn what I am writing to you, I have earned the right to write my words.

I had to understand all this information through my own worthiness, and my tears flowed – not for the excuses I have made or the experiences that I have earned, but for my children, the journey they have to make in order to understand the make-up of themselves, so that they can discover the language of their own Oracle within. I have tried to explain this to them in my own way, however, through their own conversion, they each understood it, in their own way of thinking. It is my precious grandchildren who are beginning to realize what I am saying. They are becoming eager to accept my intelligence, as their ego is equivocal – that is, in contrast to that of their parents. I am their second generation, and so equable to their right brain. Their left brain is focused on their parents, and their right brain is free to hear me.

Nothing occurs in the spur of the moment!! It has to build itself up over time to a point or an apex, which becomes an antenna of the mind. It is a derivative of the unconscious mind answering back what you are doing to yourself, and showing you the consequences that you must face in regard to the next thought. In the case of humanity, it is to the response of the emotional mind, or the language that we speak, which is where the child within (or our fear) seeks to hide for its own protection.

I am reminded here, of the times that I have walked down the street and been drawn into the shops, where I have heard a cry for help. I had to walk down the aisles to find the person who belonged to that voice. Most times, it was a Down's syndrome child, someone in a wheelchair, or otherwise disabled – so I would mirror myself to that person, and then I would leave the shop. When I returned home, I could sit in my chair with my eyes closed and tell that person a story, which they unconsciously heard. These are the sacred worlds of the Shaman. Next time I saw that same person in town, they registered to me immediately and delivered their thanks!
Your Notes:

CHAPTER FOURTEEN

We Program Our Children's Desires, Expectations, And Future Inheritance

The following chapter is not pleasant to read, yet I believe it must be written, as it is already inscribed in every one of your cells. It is known to us, through the left hemisphere of the brain, as the written word of God, or these amazing universal laws that are available, as they are instilled in every cell in our body, no one gets left out. It resides in this hemisphere in order to allow the ego to sustain itself. If I rearrange the words to explain the sentence in a different way, I am informing you of the Universal Laws that are applicable to the sentence, which resides in the right hemisphere of the brain for the emotions to reimburse the self. Both explanations have been collected through the mathematics of pure Cosmic Consciousness; it all depends on the state of mind that you are in.

The next step is for you to equate within, in order to help you understand and learn the responsibility of how to balance your mind, and also to see how you can deal with the relationship between you and your own Universal Laws – or the conversations between you and your God within. I would like to explain to you what happens to your thoughts when you are preparing to make an excuse for yourself!

Let us take our mind to the mother who aborts her child, which is becoming more apparent every day. This builds up in eclectic cycles of each thought (i.e., religious cycles, where you are returning your thoughts back to yourself so that you can understand and accept your final decision with a clear conscience), in order to show us how we are depleting and bleeding the emotional mind.

In many cases in today's world, women right around the planet are taking the lives of more than one of their own children. It has become an echo of all humanity, quietly building itself to a point where we are now just beginning to sit up and take notice. The thoughts have reached humanity's antennae, which have been struck by "God" or the "Greatest Oracle of the Divine" known today as the mathematical "Laws of the Universe", repeating back to us what we are not releasing from our past – or are refusing to understand about the growth of ourselves.

Once again, we come to the stress factor. Stress brings itself through the body when the emotional mind is bogged down, through that person's ego, overriding or sitting on the emotional mind, and thereby compressing it. The number-one fear that we all have is the failure of self. We cannot give back our emotional responsibilities to ourselves when we are being controlled by every thought, and this is what we need to remember, as our emotions cannot find the freedom to release and balance our thinking. Do you understand? Again and again, it builds and creates an altered time zone.

Not every mother wishes to have children; some even feel victimized and deprived, or feel that God has punished them – or so their story goes. Those unwanted children have stopped her from consecrating to her levels of balancing her mind – which is her Higher Self – and, therefore, she feels God is again to blame. Others just simply do not want to have children because they want their freedom in order for them to be themselves.

Another additive that I listen to and hear is the wisdom of a woman speaking, telling me that her husband is lying down on the job, and she knows, through her own intelligence, that she could create a much better life for the family than he does. She becomes very angry, and her freedom disappears. He plays the childish role, and she becomes the adult! Again, we are being reimbursed with left-brain thinking, where fear steps in here to play out its role. Over the years of child rearing, her mission to her own self-importance gets pushed further into the background, where all future hope finally disappears. In other words, she carries the responsibility of the whole family on her own shoulders. The percentage of this thinking is extremely high, and so she eradicates her children, as they are representing, futuristically, her next thought – and this she can longer bear for the fear of eradicating herself! That game usually begins in the first two years of the marriage; those first two years are the awakening of what we have committed ourselves to accept through a relationship. We come to a realization that our marriage is not what we thought it would be, and so the task of self comes through the abasement of our partner or ourselves. So, through collapsing in on herself, the children begin to appear.

We now come to the children. A child is conceived over a ninety-day gestation period of the mother coming to a fruition of self. If she fails, the pregnancy commences. The Laws of the Universe reflect back into our own Law of Self, reminding us of what we have innocently prepared through our conscious mind – but we do not have the inheritance of our own intellect to understand it! If we do not accept and use this expenditure of our thinking, the next step evolves from that. The mother has ordered, or programmed, this child through the Collective Consciousness, in order to live what she is incapable of receiving from her own higher educated mind.

Allow me to explain this story another way. When a mother symbolically represents her own child – which is through the childish attitude she is emitting to herself, through her not being able to reach a decision that she has been yearning for, she "falls" pregnant. God does not treat us too gently on this lesson, and we have no other choice than to live by it – until we learn. Her fears waylay the progress she inherits through her own acceptance of self. The story in Genesis 3:16 is, "Unto the woman he said, 'I will greatly multiply thy sorrow and thy conception; in sorrow thou shalt bring forth more children; and thy desire shall be to thy husband and he shall rule over thee.'"

We come to the point of knowing that every pregnancy is born through this behaviour. What has she programmed, through her thinking? Is it for those future children to accept the responsibility of facing up to what they must overcome, on their mother's behalf? If those children are reflecting back to her what she is too afraid to live up to regarding herself, it means that the birth of each child echoes back to the mother – that is, as to where her thoughts were leading her. Therefore, the child will realize his/ her inheritance, and then play the exact game back to what the mother could not equate regarding her thoughts to self. Did you understand this paragraph? These are also the Laws of the Universe, which are identical to the laws of God. I had a hard time earning these experiences as I had to see and understand exactly what my thoughts had programmed for each child. I flatly refused, at first, to peel the layers off my truth. It took time for me to come to terms and see it through. At that stage of my marriage, I was proud to be pregnant, and, even if I had a football team, I could always add an extra potato and a cup of water to make ends meet!

There is a snapping point, where the mind creates an antenna which is struck by the unconscious mind, just like lightning striking a tree during a storm. This is God answering back! There is nowhere for this energy to run to, as it has reached its own zenith, or its own limit, so the implosion in the mind must occur.

Who understood the problem of the mother when she had locked up her feelings of failure within herself? Who had the intelligence to understand and help her to remind herself of this precious gift of consciousness that she has already become?

Again, I am reminding you, that we are aware, that every ninety days, every cell in our body must come to a conclusion, where the mathematics of the mind kicks in to measure our thinking; so, during those ninety days of pregestation is where every woman on this earth programs, through her energy, the creation of what this "excuse" must claim to become, as a result of being human. We program our children's desires, expectations, and future inheritance through passing on to them our own instability, as well as our abilities.

Of course, you expect your children to prosper, but when their shortcomings are reflected back to you, please remember that they are mirroring you back to yourself. Have patience and tolerance to listen and help, with dignity, as you begin to "re-understand" your wisdom of self. You placed into this child your expectations of what you deemed to become. You have invited a "guest" into your home, and you are there to love and guide that child towards his/her own future. Please buy a copy of the little book, "The Prophet" by Kahlil Gibran which was written in 1929 and is still on the best-selling list, where he explains to us his interpretation on what and who are our children. Enough said!

Your children are your responsibility until they become your age intellectually or surpass you. That doesn't sound too nice, does it? By accepting this responsibility, you create a new sense of freedom for your next step, and you also allay (put to rest) the responsibility of your child.

Most mothers grow up and accept their own dilemma as each child comes along, and the next child is automatically changing her own reference library (thinking). Why? The mother's mind has "hue'n" ("Hu-An" – "tinted and coloured" - another rendition is the "heavenly understanding – through AN". "AN" is the second Metaphysical God within, known to us as our educational centre or our own Universe city) itself through her sacrifice to the relationship that she is in.

I will repeat a previous statement to reward you with. In Genesis 3:16 we read, "God spoke to Eve and said, 'I will greatly multiply thy sorrow and thy conception; in sorrow thou shall bring forth children; and thy desire shall be to thy husband, and he shall rule over thee.'" You see, when we read this, it is a totally different perception to how we read, "Go forth and multiply." God was talking about our own endeavours – our own thoughts, not the evolution of our pregnancies, which become our children. It is an explanation of the evolution of you, and also a huge lesson for humanity as a whole.

Now we can begin to understand the truth of the Bible, as well as how we are to use this information. The Bible was gathered for you to understand your thoughts. You see, God was talking to the ego of humanity, which is the left brain releasing its intelligence. The emotions that create our desires come from the vagina or the penis; it is not of the subconscious (creative or right brain). For goodness' sake, let us get this story right! It is the ego that needs religion; although, when you can believe in your own life, you will find that it has always been within you – it has just been waiting for you to come home to yourself.

One important line I wish to add here is this: The logic mind needs to create for itself the logic illusion. If we can't see it, it isn't so – it doesn't exist. For us to recognize this illusion, we must return – or retune – our energy back into understanding ourselves. It is in this section of our mind, where everything places itself into its proprietary position, which relates and cohabitates with all of our five senses. When we have brought them together, we automatically tip the scales into the next evolution, which increases the pressure and intensifies our intelligence.

There is much more I could add here – both negative and positive – but I will let you make up your own minds from now on. Just look around you, and take notice; please do not judge other women's predicaments. Women have progressed so much further than their own mothers since the last two world wars, and that progress has brought the feminine principles of all humanity up into a higher thought-form, where what we termed as "sacrifice" is becoming a thing of the past! These new women have itchy feet, and they want to accept more responsibility for themselves.

In times past, women had to learn to become both mother and father while their men were away fighting for a principle of their own and another country's standard. Just ask your grandmothers; they have a story to tell, but don't be shocked at their intelligence as they explain their story. I have listened to thousands of women as they shared their pain with me, through their fears and the hidden stories that they had trapped deliberately within themselves over their lifetimes. They don't have to lie when they are yearning to understand themselves; they just want to know the right answers to their own questions.

Your Notes:

CHAPTER FIFTEEN

The Kidneys

In my country, it is becoming more prevalent for an agreement to be drawn up between partners before they sign the marriage contract. This agreement states that no children will be born of this forthcoming relationship. These young futuristic women want to earn their freedom to enjoy their own experiences without being held responsible for rearing a family for the next twenty-one years. Are they wrong? Are they missing out on their own evolution? How were these new "seeds" of thought sown? Who put this glyph of light in their DNA? What were the hidden thoughts of their mothers in order for the next generation to prepare their lives in this way?

Look around and take notice of these "new women", many of whom have no intensions of ever even marrying! They have their minds set on a career or a life of their own exclusive royal behaviour. Are they wrong? How have we pushed consciousness up to this curve of thinking? It was through the build-up of their unconscious mind, which had gathered in the Collective and strengthened itself; this is where it has echoed out right around the planet, where it will apply itself to those women of same mind. And, as many of them have said to me, "If the world is our mirror, why should we add to the burden that we have already created? There are millions starving and millions without water, and there are millions who do not even have a home!"

This knowledge occurs not only in my country, but all around the planet, and it is voiced throughout all countries. I am here to listen to the young, as they are desperately searching to "alter the native" within themself – or are enquiring to searching for an alternative way of life. They are expecting to make a big difference in their own lives – that is, over and above what their parents have had – especially those who feel that they were deprived of their own expectations. You see, they are carrying shame, from the excuses being relayed onto them, through the innocence of their parents. God bless them. Also remember that the emotion of shame creates the dis-eases in our kidneys.

Through the mythical attention, we refer to the kidneys as "Annu", as it is pronounced throughout the Mayan and Hopi principles, in which it is explained as the supreme consciousness of the left hemisphere of the brain. It is pronounced "Anni" throughout the Egyptian philosophies, to align with equalizing the emotions of the right hemisphere of the brain. Symbolically, it represents the seed of gestation.

Throughout the mythical agenda, which we will understand as we read on, is the second dimension of God that we release: "AN" was one of the great Gods throughout the collective stories of myth. "AN" is our educational system; that is, where we learn through 'ascending and nurturing' to re-educate our self. When we understand this word through the language of the Hidden God or codes, "AN" relates to our attitude and our nourishing the self. "NU" interprets to us that, once we have nourished, we must then nurture ourselves through understanding what we have received. If taken through the Egyptian interpretation, the word, which ends with a "ni", is explaining the same thought having released its intelligence.

The word nourishment is interpreted as receiving information for the growth of self; and the word nurturing is interpreted as returning to others from the information we have already collected for our self.

We relook at the kidney area, and we now know why they have a tremendous responsibility to uphold! They must make sure that the waters of our own consciousness flow and do not become stagnant through the lack of belief in self. When we have a fear of accepting our own responsibility of self-worth, the kidneys become infected. The message from the Higher Self – or unconscious mind – is shouting back to us, "Shame on you for thinking the way you do!" They have to sort out what we are placing back into our own consciousness through us not being aware of our thinking. They cleanse the consciousness on behalf of our knowledge. Our kidneys are our "search engines", just like the ones that we use on our computers. They can either represent garments/sleeves of consciousness or create slaves for the ego's use.

Your Notes:

CHAPTER SIXTEEN

The Obese Child

Allow me to bring to your attention the obese child. There have been many parents who have become aware of my explanations on this hereditary condition, and they have come to listen to what I have had to say on the subject. They honestly had come to terms with whether they were ready to help their child – or not.

Number 1: Your child was born inheriting their parents' inner dilemma(s).

Number 2: Your child has become obese through you, the parents, not fully understanding the ability on how to digest your own thoughts.

Number 3: Through the parents' insecurity in digesting or chewing over their inner thoughts, they did not know how to nourish these empty thoughts that were not coming into fruition. They were also totally unaware that they were autonomically passing their information on to their child for their own inheritance.

Number 4: The sacred mathematical codes of the Collective are answering to us all, in one way or another – that means through the left or the right brain. The child puts on a brave face and tries to hide behind his/her insecurity. The shame of being overweight is the first step to the child's creating so many other dis-eases that have become applicable through the family's past generations, which are naturally passed on to the future generations. These are the precursors to the dis-ease of diabetes, among others.

Slowly, the mother's aggression towards the child will be brought to their attention through reimbursement, through the Collective Consciousness – i.e., that it was the mother's responsibility to her own thinking that created the difficulty in the first place. More than 20 per cent of the world's population is now creating obese children. Yes, many medical procedures are now available to help these children, but do you think that this is the only answer? How long can this monstrous attitude keep ruling our thoughts? I am explaining more than one-fifth of our global future inheritance.

More than 40 per cent of the world's population is starving and without water. What medical procedure will the child be able to have that will fix this dilemma? Any ideas out there? What is the responsibility of those people left remaining?

Thank you for listening to these words.

Your Notes:

CHAPTER SEVENTEEN

Understand Our Intelligence

There are worlds that we must complete before we can enter up into the next world. There are lifetimes that we must finish to the levels of understanding our intelligence, in order for us to be able to go forward and make our lives happen for the consideration of self – therefore, you have the ability to live many lives in this lifetime.

It's exactly the same with this quest. Remember that time and space creates the arc that Einstein speaks regarding relativity. You cannot force one of your personalities up into leading the troops, as those troops have to evolve and open themselves as well. It takes time! Allow the personality who believes in itself to lead the others to victory. If you are right, they will automatically follow you. If not, your thoughts will become scattered, and you will quickly lose what you have already gained. It is the responsibility to self that strengthens the foundations of your future.

Remember the women in previous stories? You must learn how to bring that energy back inside yourself, so that you and all those 144,000 personalities of yours (the twelve times twelve) as explained in the, 'Book of Revelations,' in the Bible, have the opportunity to procreate (produce new ideas and thoughts) as we think and rebalance our inner self as well as our outer perspectives, with one another, which will be saved.

When you finish with one world of thought, please let it be; allow yourself the privilege of creating your next world of thought through the responses of the previous one showing you the way. Let all that be in order to allow the following world to balance and come to you on its own merits, so that you can walk with yourself as one. You will find that your life is then structuring itself into a future, all by itself. The word dis-ease then has no place in your future.

I teach my students that my body is my own Universe – and, more importantly, that I am now in charge of my life, and my life is no longer in charge of me. I am also in charge of these internal organs of mine, which symbolically are representing the planets in my own solar system. My liver functions separately from my gall bladder, and it has to filter my frustrations and anger. They must work with one another, yet they are two different energies functioning and filtering the emotions that I am thinking about. My gall bladder is different from my lungs; it has to filter my vile thinking that mathematically is collecting through me not having equalized or balanced a thought. My lungs are different from my pancreas; they have to filter my breath of life.

My pancreas is there to make sure that I give back to myself the sweetness and respect of who I am. I must reward myself for the goodness that I have already created. Diabetes is the outcome if I ignore it. Diabetes is affected through my lack of sexual satisfaction making excuses to my Higher Self. I can submit to give, but I can't submit to receive.

Let me just slip another short story in here. Sugar complements our way of life, but millions died through the initial introduction of sugar into people's lives. They did not die because they ate the sugar; they died to supplement and balance the planet for those who did. In and through our innocence, we know not what we do! If those who have taken control do not release their own intelligence, the previous level of humanity must suffer. We took away the natural urge to keep ourselves loyal to self, and we introduced and created another dis-ease through releasing this reasoning. This excuse became the forerunner of diabetes.

The last organ is the spleen, which has a tremendous position to fulfil. It is the organ of balancing our truth. I think of my spleen as another planet that has to uphold the other organs; it is there to balance my whole inner Universe. It is there to hold the other organs, as well as me, upright, in order to search and accept this hidden truth, that we yearn, to learn, to earn, as each one of us prepare the mind of self, to awaken to the stories that are forthcoming from within.

From all that information, our Law of Self creates itself, and justice becomes ours. Each one of those planets – or internal organs – functions independently, yet they all have to be compatible with one another for the life force to continue.

Each of our internal organs is a separate icon, and those icons cohabitating with one another in stillness create the colour spectrum in our aura. This is the religion that we create and experience in connection with our unconscious mind; I have spoken of this before. That hidden rainbow creates itself through how we hear and prepare our thinking as to what we would like to say next. These colours earn their way through the body, evolving up to rest in the brain above our ears, and that is what we refer to as the "arching of the covenant". Again, Einstein's Theories of Relativity comes to mind.

Once we have earned this stage, all our seven seals are open. We have entered up into the section of the temple mind, where we learn to communicate and balance our thoughts with the unconscious mind. As we think our thoughts, the unconscious is there, relaying our thinking throughout the body, and we feel a centering within, where we become more tolerant and at peace with ourselves. Automatically, it is always searching for habitual resonance to help us release our freedom from a cluttered mind.

Now you can understand why the Shaman has to enter into all the worlds of consciousness to deliver the truth back to you. We must earn each energetic thought and more importantly realise, how it created itself. Where did it stem from? Our tree of knowledge is huge, and the branches are many multiplications of self.

As we begin to evolve these auric fields, the relationship to the Divine Inheritance is the colour red. Then we move into orange, yellow, green, blue, purple, and then the light opaque white. This is equivalent to the wisdom of our intelligence unfolding and creating the next level for us to evolve into. The Universe is preparing the results of our action moment by moment. Take more notice of the old masters who expressed the aura – or crown – in all its glory in their paintings. Those colours can only move forward when the previous chakra – or Seal – which is the energy of our action, has harmonized and balanced itself. This energy moves up through the vertebrae of the spine, assessing its own self-worth. This is the serpent rising; or, in Aboriginal myth, it is the Rainbow Serpent releasing itself.

So, you can see here how one unfolds the Divine Inheritance, where the vibrations are coming from a place of worthiness or the "palace of worship". To be released from the crown, that person has to become the wisdom of his/her personification of self-worthiness. The more you extol your own virtues to your God within, the more you have to continuously live up to your own expectations. Forget it! Allow it to happen naturally, through you just believing in you!

Take your time in reading my books, please, as I am delivering information to you, where there is no time – this information has been collected and formatted over many thousands of years, and this is only through the positive outcome of our thoughts divinely mathematizing themselves, which is way above and beyond what we term "time".

Your Notes:

CHAPTER EIGHTEEN

Viruses

I would like to return again to viruses: I have been initiated into this higher realm of medical sciences, through having to follow my cell's energy to watch the transference of the body's global orbit – and the consequences that I create for myself, through me not having enough confidence in my thinking.

In 1918, during the First World War, we created a bird-like flu virus through the thoughts of the Collective Mind. This virus killed around 20 million people. That number does not include the deaths of that war's participants.

In 1916, people began to notice polio, which ran rampant past the end of the Second World War. The word polio, when understood through the codes, means "through the power of the Oracle, life's intelligence is the Oracle". The crippling of the human body began, and, this time, around 50 million died. That does not include those during the war, either. This dis-ease is the result of a tithe from God for all of those men killing one another.

HIV/AIDS was created during the Vietnam War, although it began to initiate itself through the Korean War. Can you understand why this is happening? The tithing from God continues. In more recent years, we certified the corona virus. This is third-eye thinking! The SARS virus initiated itself again after 100 years of abeyance, through the bewilderment of humanity earning its intelligence, which, in turn, was through the apoplexy of our understanding of the Collective Consciousness. Again, the Laws of the Universe spoke to the people, and the tithing continues. The circle is completing itself again; through the latest virus we have named, COVID-19, and at this time, three years later we are just beginning to see the first curve begin its own spiral. Millions have passed over. As you are becoming aware of, we are not lifting our intelligence above this dilemma; all through us just not listening or not learning!

There are now 300,000 new victims of polio; but, a few years ago, we shouted to the heavens that this dis-ease had almost been eradicated from the planet.

The Ebola virus has also returned; so, somewhere along the way, we still have not learned. Whose leg are we pulling? Who is refusing to understand the consequences in regard to these Laws of the universe?

Metaphysically, Iraq interprets as "Your Ark"; or, taken even further back into our Collective, it is "UR Ark". Please remember, the difficulties the English had when transferring the Arabic language into the English understanding as the Arabic language does not have our vowels. Therefore the A_E_I_O_U was missing! Ur was one of the first recorded cities on this planet. Now could Ur, have been mistaken for - Your Ark -? Through my understanding of the Metaphysical language, the Ark is our body! No one knows for sure which city, as that knowledge has been lost as the story was passed down through the generations. Through the mathematical codes of consciousness, the name Ur means "understanding and releasing". New York is pronounced as "New Your Ark". The same name is given to the city of York in the north of England, where my family moved to just over 300 years ago from Europe. "York", "Your Ark", "UR Ark", or "New Your Ark" all depends on how someone pronounced the word to the level of their intellect – and how another then heard and interpreted it to their own level of intelligence. This is what we refer to as the "fall of Babylon". These names became cities of light, and others who were searching for expediency to their own thinking found their way to these areas to create their new home, just the same as they did thousands of years ago in Egypt.

As our intelligence has progressed, we have only just begun to accept our consequences through what is happening to us all. We are finding the courage to stand up and object to those same occurrences repeating themselves, and so we have initiated the words "I want to protest". The word protest means "to professionally test". "I want to demonstrate" and the word demonstrate means "the demon's street or strength". As we walk against one another, we are becoming aware that our thinking feeds and creates a virus, and we are all to blame. As within, so without! How does a protest march over a war create a virus to expand and feed upon itself?

In 1967, we began to protest regarding the Vietnam War, which started with around 4,000 people marching down the street; this had never been seen before. In 2003 – thirty-six years later – more than 250,000 people were walking down that same street, and millions of others in many other countries right around the world did likewise, at the same time. Still voicing the same thoughts of "Stop the War", but this time it was through the war in Iraq. As I revise my written words in 2023, this war still has no end in sight. How many people have died for your service to your belief, at that time? Is anyone listening to the outcry? I realize that many of you are offended at my words, and it is all okay with me; I am explaining how one thought is filtered around the planet, and what it can create when we are not aware of its purpose. And now we have the war in Ukraine from Russia, where again many thousands of innocent people have been killed. Their homes destroyed etc;

Take your time in digesting this chapter as I am picking up interference into what I have just written. Let us have a small rest here before I tell you another story. Your body needs to digest what you have just read. Make sure you drink plenty of water now, and it will help you adjust to the sentience of your emotional intelligence.

Your Notes:

CHAPTER NINETEEN

War

For the Vietnam War to begin, the country that stepped forward to create this debacle had to get permission from its own. It made an agreement with its government to allow that energy to flow, so the war proceeded and began to grow. Humanity then began to notice what that war was creating. Young men were dying, cities were destroyed, and women and children were massacred and injured by the thousands. Not just their houses, but the homes where they lived and breathed, we destroyed, and we, humanity, watched as their lives were blown apart. Did those innocent people really understand what was going on?

We started to feel that war within ourselves, through the power of television being broadcast into our homes. We could see what was happening, and we took part in that war, emotionally. Because it could enter into our own resting place, we became guilty much more quickly. Why? As we sat down to watch the news, we saw the horrors of war being broadcast directly into our own lounge rooms, and this did not appease us. It set the Alchemy of our own brain into action, and we began to get irritated with everything much more quickly. The war invaded our homes, and our emotional mind became troubled; that affected our inner territory, and it began to interfere with our way of life.

National Service called the young men of my country to protect it, and so our sons signed up through the call of their innocence, sacrificing but not surrendering to the Elders of the tribe. Before they signed the consent form, they had volunteered their lives, not their selves, in service to their country. They were searching for an additive in order to bring themselves into their eclectic responsibility.

My heart filled with love for those National Servicemen, as their thoughts tried to understand the what, when, where, and why in the aftermath of the Vietnam War. I have listened to the fears of those young men whose thoughts are gathered throughout the Collective Consciousness, and I have saluted the decisions that they made to complement themselves.

Young people still join the military services today, and it is their way of measuring up to their own responsibilities; to be disciplined into entering up into their higher mind. This is only until they understand, through their personal experiences, their own self-worth. Their fear of death can become a challenge for them to overcome – a challenge that comes from deep within. The Warrior births his wisdom through the adrenalin rush that releases through the expectations of his own achievement.

I am speaking to you here through the myth of stories that have been handed down through the generations; stories of the explanation of the first God, known to us through the codes as "EL". Read the mythical stories of the God "EL", and you will see how this is reflected back to us from the Collective as the symbolic God who controlled the sexual doorway. It is only through this doorway of consciousness that war can eventuate. That doorway is where we learn to release our inner urges, where we find the inner strength and power that will push us forward.

I have listened to hundreds of stories from men who fought in various wars; they come to me to set their mind free. They attend my seminars to receive an explanation as to why they were deprived of the fulfilment of their own gestation! Shame is the collector of their emotions, and shame leads to many dis-eases which start in the kidney area and affect the prostate gland. When the prostate becomes dis-eased, it ridicules the sexual satisfaction one still hopes to receive. This creates a relationship with the adrenals, arising from an innocent childish outbreak of expectations. We fill our mind with doctrines that have been handed down through the generations, and when we become ashamed of those experiences, it affects the endocrine system. Those men do not die in vain.

We have grown up since the Second World War. There was no TV then, only radio, and the news was three weeks old by the time we received it. So, we appeased our own emotional self; innocently, we had already prepared our emotional mind for the worst. Today it is sitting right in front of our eyes; it is in our sight, on a daily basis, as we come home to rest at the end of the day.

A war takes around twenty-five years to begin to earn its place of endowment, and three years to collect the inheritance of our thinking, which is a total of (4 x 7= 28) twenty-eight years to manifest itself, which represents a generation of humanity's growth. If we go back through past history, we can see the portentous game we have revealed to the rest of humanity, through us striving for our own expectations to urge the world into becoming free. War cannot manifest overnight, and consciousness collects on our behalf; after which, it must step in again to create the plans for us to be rewarded to obtain our future. Please also remember that time is accrued only through and for the left brain, as it fears the progress of taking full responsibility for its thinking.

The fear tactic that we create springs to attention before we have accepted our own responsibility, and so we have an urge to protest. This must coerce through the mind of the initiates, taking over the responsibility of their consequences, by which the rest of us must then abide.

Look at the grotesque shapes that form as we watch the smoke swathes from exploding bombs. These smoky forms look like the heads of monsters. Yet these same forms – these "smoke signals" – are created and reflected back to us from the Collective Inheritance as to what we are creating for others and ourselves.

So, when you begin to protest against what your government is doing, you are arguing with your Higher Self. "Not on!" says God. Did the government give you permission to try to stop this war? No, it did not! You made this appeasement through your own thoughts, yearning to soothe the hostility that was building up within you.

Treat this paragraph with care, as you can see how this story begins to reflect back to you in regard to how HIV/AIDS multiplied itself through the demonstrations of marching against the Vietnam War. How did we begin to feed the corona virus? Don't forget the bird flu or SARS. A chicken cannot fly higher than 13 feet, as that altitude is the bird's zenith; therefore, they have become a species that must sacrifice to us. They did not protest; they became the victims of what the protesting was creating for the rest of us. All this information is just one cell of the eternal species, explaining to us the inner performance of the Collective of the Consciousness or the mathematical collection of the Universal Laws.

Throughout the language of Shamanism, a viral thought must combust itself through reaching its own zenith. It starts as an irritation to the mind (just as an insect is an irritation to our senses), which is measured throughout the body before it dissolves through its own energy realizing itself. The more advanced we become, the more we move through multiple worlds in our mind – and we learn to live at the point of conception, which is where our evolution keeps unfolding itself. This allows the mind to live in its freedom permanently.

I would like to introduce you to the word tithe. Tithing is a Metaphysical response to the higher, heavenly mind. It is a code of adjustment or payment made to the Divine response – or the Collective Consciousness – of everything we say or do. No! We cannot take it away or ignore it; it is the evolution of the body language of our own Collective Consciousness in regard to how we have learned to think and speak our thoughts. The Universal Law states that 10 per cent of everything that we create must be tithed; this is a mathematical code that has been delivered to us through the ancient Law of Responsibility. Tithing is an expectation to the changes one makes when one commits to something. This is our payback to God. If God is not satisfied with our result, we have to walk backwards until we right the wrong that we have already done. The explanation of the number ten (1), through the Sacred Numerology means this: "Through the changes I have made, I will accept and move on to the next higher realm of accepting my Soul (0)." That is the reason for the tithe of 10 per cent. It has nothing to do with money

Through everything we create – whether it is in singular or group force – once it is set in motion, the tithing releases through the Divinity. As this accrues, the mathematics set the holographic imprint to what we have created, and the tithing then continues without human intervention. We must, therefore, pay our dues of 10 per cent of every thought that we have created back into the Collective. Once we have reached 10 per cent, the Collective takes over and automatically corrects the energy of the planet.

That story also explains how every dis-ease is created. This is the open doorway that leads you onward to the next evolution of yourself. You have created that dis-ease in your mind through an additive of your thinking, where you have collected the poison one drop at a time. That dis-ease, that repetition of self, has taken on its own life force and overpowered you. You can now either give in to the dis-ease, or think positively and thank the dis-ease for showing you your mistakes. Through tithing back to self, you have the opportunity of healing yourself. God has never made a mistake.

Your Notes:

CHAPTER TWENTY

Body Language

My training into body language began through the teachings of what the Shamanic philosophies refer to as the "Hidden God". My training all began with an itch. An itch is an irritation reflecting out through the senses to connect with its outer boundary, which is the surface of the skin. It is given back to us from the thoughts we are busily creating and thinking within. Instead of scratching myself, I had to learn to touch the itch no matter where it was situated (the importance of where it collected throughout the body evolved later) – and I also had to learn to say "thank you" to the itch. I had to surrender to the itch, brush my hand over it, and pull it away from my body. Lo and behold, once I learned how to do this, the itch stopped! What was this? It seemed so simple and easy. Where did it go? How did it dissolve? Did it transfer itself elsewhere into the body? My skin began to repair itself once I accepted and understood this unconscious reaction, which became a lesson I never forgot. In other words, through my thoughts, my thinking was being mirrored back to me.

I began to realize that I was communicating with another realm of my intelligence. I was stepping up into the language of the unconscious mind, which I now refer to as my "Unified Consciousness". I had been running the same old movie of repeating the thought over and over again, and I would not let it go. I was afraid to step out. I was being dragged out of my own safety net through this understanding – so much so that I was irritated through all of my senses.

Over the next few years, I learned to understand every cell in my body, its program, and what its responsibility was to keep me moving forward. These were the years of no sleep and no eating; I did not need any of that. I fed myself through my own wisdom being reimbursed back to me.

I have one book to thank for this introduction into my new life: You Can Heal Your Body by Louise Hay. I read that book and protested, and then I read it again and demonstrated. I read it for a third time, as I finally began to understand where she was coming from. I found my inner government, and I marched forward to release my own peace. I realized that I was tapping into the autonomic responses of my own central nervous system. That was how I began to understand my Hidden God within; it was speaking back to me telepathically.

When we understand that the brain functions totally in the language of the unconscious mind – or the Metaphysical language – we can begin to reveal the Oracle of our make-up. In that way, we can serve ourselves through a religious experience being construed back through us, which is then reflected on an outer level. We must stop trying to control ourselves through holding onto the past, as this blocks our emotional inheritance and holds us back into its abeyance. How can the light come through our cells when we hold it back? Once we know and accept the language of self, we open up the space to think clearly. Over and over, I recalled my grandmother's words: "Aim for the highest; there is room at the top."

My next step was to learn about pain. Pain is felt in this moment – whether it is past or present pain. We are responsible for our own pain through us creating it, all by ourselves. There is no one else to blame! Pain creates itself only through the thinking of the left brain, so we deal with it the only way we know how. Through our own ignorance, we don't understand how to come to terms with our pain, and so we search for something – or someone – else to take it away.

Pain is created through the build-up of the five senses coming together. It is an echo of instability, which, again, is given back to us through our Higher Self. In other words, we are not listening to the repetition of our thoughts. Through our understanding of that power within, both brains can be retrained. When we can ascend through our inner levels, we can begin to feel the gathering of our own power, rather than the trapped emotions or the fear. I remembered an old saying of my father's, when I was a child, about the word can coming before the word cannot!

You are in control of yourself, so you must find the courage to learn to retrain your responses in order to teach and believe in yourself. Nobody else can do that for you. You cannot place your responsibility onto someone else; that is automatically halving your intellect. I seem to be harping about the same subject all of the time, don't I? All of which is the written word, throughout the Bible and especially in the Book of Revelations. Simply put, repetition is the answer. Grow up and begin to accept what you have created for yourself. You have to learn to step into your pain and regraft the wisdom you have earned back into your self – and accept that you did this, all by yourself. Stop using a crutch for your own demise.

In the moment that I had created a pain, I had to touch it with my right hand and burp, and that burp then began to release the pain that I was in. The more I burped, the less intense the pain became. The wonderful world of Chinese medicine has been explaining this to us for thousands of years, so learn to understand how their medicinal knowledge heals their body. It was not easy for me to accept this method, until I began to realize that, through burping, the energy was reshaping itself. Burping was going against my childhood upbringing – where women just did not do that sort of thing – and so I took to closing all the doors in the house, hoping that nobody heard me and trusted that the pain would release itself. It worked! It was similar to learning what I needed to do in order for the itch to release itself.

The moment a pain diminished I knew that the energy had transformed itself. Burping releases yesterday; it releases our blocked energy and fear, which is that locked-in emotion we like to ignore. If we release the energy of pain, it must relinquish, as it can no longer feed upon itself. No energy, no life force. I teach this method now in many countries around this wonderful globe, and become aware of thousands that have benefited.

When we burp, we become our own Alchemist. We release a chemical action that has been created on behalf of our thoughts in order to give our brain the opportunity to refurbish our cellular structure. Remember that the brain can only communicate through the unconscious energy of our thinking. Those chemicals are greatly enhanced by the arcing

(Ark-King) of our own covenant, through the respect that we return to the higher mind or "helm".

Your Notes:

CHAPTER TWENTY ONE

The Disease You Create

Dis-ease is created by your body fluids objecting to the thought that you have in your moment. The dis-ease you create, be it genetic or not, depends on how you carry that thought. Genetic inheritance is an explanation of understanding our energetic evolution. Of course, all this can – and will! – change when we bother to concern ourselves with the design we have inherited of our self-worth. When you find the strength and courage to understand yourself, the solution is very simple. Go to your medical doctor, or alternative practitioner, and know, in your own mind, that you are ready to deal with the dis-ease.

Earning your free will means that you have the possibility of bringing in your dark or light force at any given moment. The dark force is your required strength which travels up through our DNA, and the light force is your acquired intelligence which comes down from above through our DNA. We are offered this choice of conformity through the left and right hemispheres of the brain, at the moment when they begin their life force, joining at the stem of our brain, which actually begins just above our hips. The comprehension of your actions comes through the result of the final measurement, which is all in the control of the master system: the pituitary gland.

A dis-ease is of the same mind as we are – it is a replica of our genetic inheritance. Darkness cannot work without the light; so, if we cannot believe in ourselves, this dis-ease must complete its own life force. Through not believing in ourselves, we give our dis-eases free rein – and it will reign supreme because we allow it to do so.

Here are a few questions and answers that may assist you in answering your questions.

Question: When I have a pain, I place my hand on it, and burp. I have understood that. But do I not have to go to the original thought that has created this pain within me?

Answer: That original thought was what you believed to be your truth at that time, and your truth is something that you earn. It is the builder of the parliament of your three consciousnesses, and it is buried deep within your DNA. Through Egyptian philosophy, it is the mind of Ma'at, which is the justice one earns for the self. This is the birthing of the angel within.

If you clear the energy, the mirror – or memory – autonomically comes to you. To release itself, the thought that created the pain must mirror itself back to you. This does not come through you searching for it! Let this blockage find its own judicial wisdom through its own possibilities of clearing itself, and it will never return back to you.

This is the first step to your own sanctification. Your sainthood is building its own requirements within – through releasing itself. While you are burping, you are already concentrating on yourself. Go to your mind. Watch as the thought that created the pain shows itself through a Metaphysical resonance. This is what the vision world is all about.

Metaphysics is the language of the waking dream state. Your unconscious mind is communicating back to you, so watch closely as the memory returns. It may not remind you instantly of the problem, as you must realize that this is through the unconscious mind revealing a myth or parable back to you in story form, where you have the chance to catch up, to unravel the lessons that come from your higher domains. If you are a beginner on your way to accepting this information, then your Higher Self will reflect your story back to you in a childlike manner. The more you comprehend this inner language, the stronger the message that you will receive.

Every myth which has been passed down to you through your previous generations is still here in service to you. The reason for this is through you realizing that you have still not understood the original message. I used to react to someone else's intelligence when they said to me, "Oh, it is just a myth, so don't worry about it; it is just a fantasy." Well please think again; it is time for all of us to reinvest in those myths! It is like a nightmare you have that wakes you up; you do not understand it, and so, in your panic, you turn away from yourself. It is through your innocence that you do not want to know about it. I do not want to keep on writing the word ignorance! Come and sit in my class for a few months and learn to earn your next commitment to self.

All this information is the explanation of a Metaphysical resonance. Pain is created in the body from your unconscious extolling its virtues back to your conscious thought (your ego or fear) of what you are not learning or accepting regarding yourself. Therefore, pain is continuously recurring when you are not in attendance to your own thoughts. Please, let's change your molecular structure! Don't forget to say those three magic words: "I thank me!"

Question: I suffer with terrible pain in my lower back and thighs during ovulation and menstruation. I feel sick and want to vomit for one week before my period begins, and it makes me so angry that I just want to scream!

Answer: Ah, yes, this is a big one for those women who are emotionally locked in. It would have started to interrupt you in the beginning of your puberty, and also would have been a problem to your mother and grandmothers as well. Now don't become offended by this answer, but it usually has to do with the relationship between a daughter and her father. It is a standoffish relationship with an untold story between the conscious and subconscious minds. The young girl becomes offensive to what her father is insinuating on a hidden level. His power becomes connected to her emotionally, through what he expects of her, and how he expects her to behave and relate to others. It is an inner incest of the Soul. This lowers her hormone levels, and she becomes detached from her Higher Self.

That connection grows and accrues through the unconscious collection of both father and daughter's thoughts. In other words, God is returning her pain back to her in order to alert her to the fact that she is shutting the door on her own emotional mind.

She reflects a "tomboy" attitude and turns her back on herself. That detachment of self continues as she becomes a woman, and the pain continues to collect each month. Her own bodily functions are in abeyance, waiting for her to accept the reproduction of her old thinking by changing her attitude. Her anger and frustration build over the cycle, in trepidation of the period that she does not want to have. The woman is not at home in her mind, so she does not allow her positive energy to flow; the little girl is still locked into her past fear, so she shuts the door to the inner moan within.

Now come with me while I introduce you to an answer on a higher level. Females who are born on the equatorial circle of the planet have a different system; they receive their period at an earlier age and it lasts longer than those who are born in the northern or southern hemisphere. Why is this so? Their unconscious mind lives within the tilt of the planet; which means that they are in a near zero activation of the magnetic waves. This is what we refer to through Metaphysics as the Divine or Heavenly Activation of Thought. They do not have to think too much, and they can't – the energy of the planet does not allow that to occur. That equatorial area is referred to as a Cosmic "time warp". Many people choose to take their holidays in that area, so that they can totally relax and slow their bodies down to a compatible resonance. Are they gaining or losing during this time? The people from the north and south are gaining equilibrium to their thinking, and the equatorial people are losing their opportunities to evolve.

As the sun is to the Universe, so it is with the solar disc that is autonomically created within each human brain. This light manifests through the release of its own strength as our intelligence unfolds itself. This, through the Egyptian prophecies, is the birth of the "Rah". It starts with the light waves that are correlated up through the spine when we are standing upright. Those waves then travel through the intelligence of our thoughts and up through the vertebrae, to equate the menstruation – or periodic cycle – with the gestation of our thoughts.

Women are all born with this inheritance from mother to daughter, and it also occurs from father to son. Please do not think that a man is devoid of a periodic explanation of his thinking. Emotionally, he goes through what we women take for granted, although it reacts slightly differently with men. They get caught up in their emotional mind and can't find their strength during this cyclic event. My male students and I have tested this over the years, and, through their own research and my information, they come to perfectly understand what I am referring too, and then they are able to move on. They like to refer to it as "stress".

The equation for women's cycle is 4 x 7 = 28 (days). We need to receive the inner nurturing for self-fulfilment, and this is created through the breasts. The equation for men's cycle is 6 x 7 = 42 (days). This is to the attunement of their testicles, through which they master their own expectancy of self- worth. Those hormones also need self-assertiveness.

It is when we can attune our self, more into our own vibration – and walk away from our tribal law in the mind – that this system can then change our attitude. And this gives us the possibilities to re-create our own tribal law – our Law of Self. Our birthing higher up into this next level of the family tree coincides with the illumination of the solar disc – or the light of our self-manifestation within. This is the prophecy of self, lifting us up into the freedom that we are given, through the universal Law, to use for ourselves. Do not look at the sun; it is too bright and it will blind you – look into your own brain instead, as this is the storehouse for your light!

Question: My husband has had lower back problems for many years. Can you please explain to me in your language how this is created?

Answer: Over 99 per cent of back problems belong to people who are too afraid to believe in themselves. They are mentally sitting down on the job, looking for excuses. Lower back problems begin in your heels under the ankles and travel up to the hip area; this is the sciatic nerve area – or the Upper Kingdom, as it is explained through the hieroglyphs of the Egyptian law. When we walk on tiptoe, our heels are not on the ground, so we are refusing to understand ourselves. The sciatic nerve comes to a completion under the heel around the Achilles tendon, which is biblically known to us as the readings of the "Arcing of Elias" tendon.

I enjoyed unravelling the codes in the Bible to see how each story is a Metaphysical explanation as to how the human body created itself. I would love to explain these codes in the stories of the Bible relating to Eli, Elias, Elija, or Elisha the High Priest, who was sent out into the desert to understand his Spiritual law; while in the desert, the ravens fed him. Eli was fed through the species that was passed through him, which is his own sacred law (and that is the raven) – that is, where he had to begin to believe in himself. As his intellect evolved and opened up his inner dictionary, his name changed from Eli the innocent, to Elija the ego. This change happened in order to release his intelligence. Once he understood his quest, his name changed again, and he became Elisha. This is in the name of the Shah – or his Higher Self –and the stories continue.

Let us get back to the lower back; it is all the same story. That lower back pain is also created through a sexual molestation of self, from the left brain to the right brain. Your husband is deliberately shutting down the temple door or the "sky attic" to his own Godhead.

Please ask him to be honest with himself through admitting this: "I have a fear of accepting my life, as I will refuse to believe again, that my pain is my own demise." Ask him to bring that knowledge into his cellular construction company – where he is constructing his own thoughts – and he will have the privilege of understanding which cell is out of alignment.

You cannot fly high if your wings are still dragging on the ground. You cannot sail the ocean of all, through your anchor being caught up on a rock on the shore. Stop making excuses to – and for – yourself.

Maybe now, by accepting what I have just explained to you, your husband can release his pain. His pain is his own creation, and it will last as long as he turns his back on himself. Pain is a part of you processing your own intelligence; pain is a fear caught up in its own control. Pain can only relay itself inside your body through the lessons that the left hemisphere of your brain still has to succumb to.

Question: My father has just been told that he has Parkinson's dis-ease, and he is only forty-two years old. There is no history of this dis-ease in our family. How do you explain this?

Answer: Ah yes! Well, I explain things a little differently than others do. Take heart, because there is much happening with this dis-ease. The dedication of the medical research is culminating a part of the answer. The alternative institutions are also making this dis-ease a top priority; they, too, have a part of the answer. This dis-ease had itself up to warrant a "top priority" position. Personally, I sometimes use the fields of radionics to help those patients who have difficulties in understanding my way. They arrive full of hope, but their fear stands in front of them while they appear before me, trying to ask for advice through finding the confidence to reach up for the benefits of the so-called alternative.

One thing I do know is that the codes are the "be all to end all". No human or machine in existence can match this Divine Intelligence – at least, not at this time. Let me explain the "pendulum effect", which has been here since time began, and which is still in use to this day, even in our space programs.

The codes of homeopathy – which are measured on the wavelengths of the energy compounded in plants, etc., and which comprise the root race of the Collective – all still hold the keys to the wisdom which we have forgotten and for which we are still searching. Those codes of energy are then brought through and measured into a numerical format. A series of mathematical numbers are the Soul number of that species, and they have an extra dimension that they can use through time. Their senses have evolved towards the emotions of exception, and that is something that does not follow the general rule, as we know it today.

They must equate and learn to balance through their sensing of their own bodily functions. So it is, exactly the same reasoning for the next generation of evolution; there is no difference throughout the Laws of the Universe. We are measured by our reasoning, which is our own intelligence understanding itself through our DNA.

I program a crystal or a piece of plastic with the appropriate homeopathic resonance to suit this dis-ease. Then I ask the patient to carry this on the body – or in a pocket, wallet, handbag, etc., – and allow the vibrations to work on their behalf, while learning, most importantly, that they must accept their consequential relationship to this dis-ease that they allowed to proceed. The crystal or plastic that I program for these patients can also be placed in the trouser pocket of the man, or nestled into the bra of the woman. There is a reason for this. The man's trouser pocket is in alignment with his testicles, which represent the nourishing of self, so the ego is satisfied. The woman's bra is in alignment with her breasts, which represent the nurturing of self, so the emotions can realign. Therein is a reminder of the beginning of balance for each of us. My father had his crystals in his trouser pocket for 60 years, and when his left lung was removed through Granular Mitosis, he transferred those crystals to his shirt pocket and yes, you have guessed it, he grew it back again.

It is amazing how many people want alternative medicine; although I like to inform them that sometimes the alternative way is not as easy as taking medication. The alternative comes through a meditation of the mind, where we have more potency through a greater belief of self. They want to "alter the native" from deep within themselves. This is a new way for them to adjust to – and, think about it, this is not like the medication most people are accustomed to taking _– it is not a tablet or capsule that they just put into their mouth and swallow. You will find that, once the same issue keeps recurring, it means that the patients want to know more information regarding themselves. This is where the psychotherapist steps in to remind them of their old ways; that now must be brought into an order.

They need to release this inner courage that is in the wings ready to serve them; they need to learn to trust in their own inner strength in order for this method to work, and then they will notice that the changes will begin to occur straight away. I ask them to keep a diary to record, three times each day, what their emotions are reflecting back to them.

Parkinson's dis-ease is building into a stronger dis-ease than it was ten years ago, and it has now become life threatening, so it is to these patients' benefit to take part in the opportunity to help themselves.

So let us take your father's dis-ease "Parkinson" through the codes. "Pa- Ark-Inn-Son" – now let me explain this story to you. "Pa" means father. "Ark" means your body, "your ship within", your Noah's Ark; arcing itself, step by step, into the unconscious or higher mind. "In" relates to our inner nurturing, inner self, or resting place – or Bethlehem in the Bible. "Son" means strength of one's self. Thus, the word Parkinson means: "As my power ascends throughout my ark, and I rest myself within, I then pass on my responsibilities to the next generation." That is what the dis-ease is all about. How does that story sound to you?

Parkinson's dis-ease is created when the energy in the body begins to reach its zenith, through the inner vibrations of thoughts, creating a form of jealousy over someone or something other than self. Anger then starts to collect itself up into the thinking, and, as this power ascends, our attitude begins to change. This places tremendous responsibility on the muscular involvement, which, in turn, echoes throughout the organs and changes their frequency to vibrate beyond their normal expectations. The arcing of the intelligence that he should be in touch with is not working through him to become a benefit to his mind. The energy collected in the body has been automatically pushed up beyond its own recognition, and it becomes absent through its lack of will; stubbornness then moves in to take its place in the game. In most cases, when taking my clients who have this dis-ease back down their path of collective memories, they can all agree with these findings.

Let us look at the end of verse 4 of the 23rd Psalm: "Thy rod and thy staff, they comfort me." Well, the person with Parkinson's has the rod in order but has no staff to comfort themself. In Egyptian law, we call this the hook and the flail. If we notice the symbology, the Pharaoh holds the staff in his left hand – and, when we are totally controlling our self, there is no one home to deliver the sentence. The staff is there to pull us back when we overstep our mark through all of these previous aggressions building upon each together. This psalm is in relationship to the thyroid gland ("Thy-Roid"). The word roid, in the ancient English language, means "stiffening up the dregs of the past, which create aggravation."

There are many ways of helping your father; but, first, he must want to help himself. It takes about eight years for this dis-ease to seat itself throughout the body, and, when he is ready for help, the right person will be placed there to show him his way to the level of his understanding. When he has accepted that, he can move up to the next teacher, and so on.

Thank you for your question! Now, please release the pressure in your mind, and simply love your father, as your love will help him release the pressure of his mind – and this is all he needs right now; he does not need your worry.

CHAPTER TWENTY TWO

The Temple Mind

The Book of Psalms, when understood through the Metaphysical, is the temple mind – that is, your forehead, and this is the home of the prophets, or your vision worlds. This is the home of David, or "Davidya" (if we look further back in history, it was pronounced as "Davidea") through the ancient language of the Sanskrit, which is the Indian philosophy; it is the inner screen. We place a video into a machine, and then we turn on the TV and the screen comes alive. King David the prophet releases and sends praises back into our body through the world of visions, allowing the tension of the body to release through the body's own accord.

Here are a few questions and answers that may assist you in answering your questions.

Question: I have had a very bad cold for a long time, and my body is still wracked with pain. What does that mean?

Answer: The common cold is a wonderful story, and it begins through you objecting to know, see, or hear yourself. Three of the five senses become blocked: one from each evolution of the mind of self. You are living your life in your moment, but you are not paying too much attention to yourself. In other words, either you are sacrificing yourself to others, or you are draining the inner wisdom by bleeding yourself dry. Your thoughts are not your own; you are giving them away. This builds up inside your cells, the mucous starts to become phlegmatic, and your body slows down.

Go back over your last ninety days to see how the tithe from the Higher Self has had to show you what you have created. It is an echo of what you have done to yourself. Remember these next few sentences. Having a cold is a Spiritual cleanse in order for the body to release on an inner level. Can you accept this cold through accepting that you will regain your free will? Yes, you can, when you have reminded yourself once again how important you are to you. That clears and releases the pressure in the cells, and, once this is complete, it has the opportunity to heal itself.

Adults usually get a cold during the winter months. Why is this? As the temperature drops from the warmth of the summer months, the body has to reclaim the freedom that it found for the excuses that we make for ourselves during that warmer existence. This is to prepare our mind for the next step up into achieving our intelligence. If we did not have a viral attitude to our own self-acclaim, we would not have had to receive a cold. Remember that the higher our intelligence evolves, the colder the temperature the body needs for its own success.

Children begin to cleanse during the spring and autumn months. They need to cleanse during those seasons to prepare for the strength of the summer months and the endurance of the winter. The polarities of their small bodies cannot take on the full responsibility until their nervous systems have unfolded intellectually to support their highest degree. It takes three cycles of seven years each for the immune system to activate into its fullness. By wrapping our children up warmly during the winter, we are giving sanctuary to their sixth sense – for their later evolution. My doctor students were quite amazed, when we started to research and study these phenomena, and found all this to be so.

Remember the story of the immune system? The first seven years is for the birthing of the endocrine system, the next seven are for the immune system to awaken, and the final seven years are for the lymphatic system to seat itself over all (the "Overlord").

Can we cure the common cold? I hope not! We will just place another veil over what we have refused to understand up to this point, and another strand of the dis-ease will always begin to create itself throughout the Collective Consciousness. We have a fair way to go yet before we understand this game, but it will come to its own completion through all of us discovering the intelligence to enter into a higher order.

Question: I have a female patient who has just had a heart

transplant. She wants alternative healing, so could you explain this to me metaphysically, please?

Answer: Our heart fails us through our not paying attention to the joy that we are able to create for self; in other words, we are not respecting our own self-worth. Our heart is the inner battery of our vehicle, and if it is not checked every now and again by the right brain, which is our emotional responsibility to self, it begins to run dry. The battery takes distilled water to keep it running, and when we are energized emotionally, our heart needs the same attention.

The heart of your patient was removed through her squeezing all the joy out of her life, and she followed in her parent's footsteps; she was clutching her heart too hard with her left hand. Another person's heart was transplanted into her, and, if she continues on and is still hanging onto the same old thinking, the new heart will also begin to flicker and create the same old fear in her again.

The alternative she needs right now is her own thinking – through revaluing and returning her attention back to herself. This is the reason that most women have a different form of heart attack than men have. They are so busy playing everyone else's game, and they have difficulties in finding enough respect within to live their own life.

It is the same with the disease cancer. I have had many cases where I have done healings, and, in the beginning, I had to explain to the patient why the cancer manifested in his/her body. The power of the mind is the most sensitive instrument on the planet. I took each patient back to the point where the original thought created itself, and they each were able to see why the first cell became blocked. Most patients went into remission as they began to hear their past thoughts, because they then understood their quandary. Some of them died a few years later through that cancer manifesting elsewhere in the body; the cancer came back through the thinking that created it in the first place, where the thoughts were still locked in. They listened, but they could not hear. It never returned to the place where it was healed; it chose the next-weakest organ in connection with the thought in order to re-create its new life force.

Your Notes:

CHAPTER TWENTY THREE

Love Is The Oracle Of Life

There is one positive emotion on this planet, and that emotion is love – all other emotions are leading up to love. Love is the "Oracle of Life"; it is energy in motion, and that is what holds our DNA together. Remember, we earn love, which manifests throughout the body and releases our truth. It is a condensed formation of what is hidden within us all. Through the power of our inner self understanding itself, our freedom extends to become everlasting life.

Symbolically, we have twelve strands in our DNA, and those strands are coiled in a double helix and held together by the strand of emotion. Twelve strands come up the body to represent the fear instilled in the left brain (our logic), and twelve come down from above to support the emotions in the right brain (our emotion). Do you remember the stories told through mythology of the six dark lords and the six lords of light? Emotions of love are much stronger than fear, and it is emotion that holds us together. Our body falls apart when we turn our back on our emotions, all through the ego running amok.

Allow me to bring to your attention to another problem that we are still releasing to humanity, and this is the difficulties that we have with cloning. The people who clone cannot achieve the twelfth strand of DNA, and this is the key to the freedom of the cells – this is what creates the life force and makes the body grow. That twelfth strand is connected to the Soul! We should have learned all this through the sheep that they called Dolly. Be careful with this new science! We need to understand that God places the responsibilities here for us to nourish ourselves so that we have the possibility to nurture one another. We have made enough genetic mistakes already.

I would like to explain another difficulty that we need to bring to humanity's attention, and that is about the mind of many parents who have brought in vitro fertilization (IVF) children into the world. The percentages of success are not very satisfactory; according to my resources in London, there are now less than 5 per cent of cells that connect with the sperm. The reason for that is very simple; they do not want to. They do not belong to this backward thinking, and they cannot go back into an excusable excuse.

Stop trying to make an excuse for the ego – it is here to earn its fulfilment; it is not here just to yearn! It has already grown up! There is a huge separation between you and the Collective Consciousness of God here!

The statistics are quoted as saying that only 1.5 per cent of results are satisfactory. Something is wrong here. These children born through an IVF program have many difficulties to overcome as to how they can learn to function emotionally with their intelligence. So far, there has not been one child recorded with an equable balance, and the parents have become very frustrated trying to understand their child's behaviour. They want to know how to cope with these situations in order to ease the stress and burdens in the family life. The parents have collapsed into their child within; and their own intelligence does not know how to keep walking backwards on itself. We think we have the God-given right to alter what we have already become. These blessed children need extra guidance and comfort; they need to feel emotionally balanced thoughts coming from their parents, not their frustrations! This program is new to our thinking, so let us understand how we can benefit these children and allow them to accomplish their own emotional endeavours. May I say today as I revise and add my latest information that there has been a great change to the IVF treatment.

If a woman does not become pregnant, it is with good reason – and it is through the design of her Collective Inheritance. Not everything can be created in a test tube – thank God! It is only through the ego demanding its own glory that we have created these misdemeanours in our life. That woman has a program that has collected up to this point over many generations, and she must accept this, and then she can begin to live.

Let's take a look at which partner wanted the IVF – was it he or she? If it was the male, then why could he not find his own satisfaction and release himself to her? Or, was it the woman looking for what she could not find within herself, and so she tried to impose the IVF onto him – or vice versa? Are they happy in this relationship? Which one is the leader? Which one is the sacrifice? Which one is the martyr? I can go on and on asking these impertinent questions. Throughout the northern hemisphere, a tremendous amount of IVF parents exists, and they are creating self-help groups in order to share their burdens. We have created another "tribe", where all are desperate to understand their emotional inheritance.

Learn to read your own codes of what and who you have become! Stop looking for your own excuses, and, for God's sake, trust in what you have achieved through birthing your intelligence to nurture your own mind. Children are born through a childish attitude to satisfy our ego, not our emotions. Always remember that the child births the child.

If you cannot become pregnant, a greater reason exists in order for this to have come through your DNA. You are here on this planet from your parent's expectations, and, when you have achieved and given that glory to self, you will then be free in the mind and able to help others. Your responsibility is to share with those who cannot help themselves. In the presence of God, you are an angel. Your intelligence has delivered to you this warranty of self- worthiness on a platter, and your codes have accrued to the responsibility of your intelligence. Bless yourself and be thankful for the appreciation of your tribal law. You are on the way to becoming an Elder.

We are beginning to understand the Arcing of the Covenant that is made between each one of us and God. I love the word in the German language, which is the Bundeslade or the "Larder of Abundance".

Your Notes:

CHAPTER TWENTY FOUR

Men's Problems

Question: I have a long-time problem. As a teenager, I had difficulties with my testicles; they seemed to be hidden for many years, and, when they finally dropped, one grew larger than the other. One fills up with fluid all the time. Has this to do with my prostate? My father had prostate problems. I went back into my family tree through your teachings, and found that my grandfather did not have these symptoms. He had hernias around the navel, and they were operated on periodically. Can you help me to understand myself?

Answer: My beautiful young man, if I can give you the right explanation, I will have helped thousands of men with the same problem. Let us go back into your Tree of Knowledge of Good and Evil, and begin with your grandfather. Men are very prone to Hernias. Allow me to inform you that this is through the implanting of the DNA not being recognized emotionally. It is where the ego was fed through the stubbornness that had collected, generation after generation, through the restrictions they placed on their mind. They did not know intellectually how to fix their regenerative tissue, as their thoughts were passed on to their sons; and, when this did not happen, the tissue became weaker.

Your grandfather inherited his hernias through the past generations of his ego urging itself beyond the belief of its own intelligence. The ego flatly refuses to listen to any goodness or worthiness about the self. His thoughts were of hard work; the more he had to do, the better he worked. Their thoughts were, "What I can do today, I can do double tomorrow." It is passed on to the next inheritance through the mind continually yearning for release from this dictator that has taken over the inner thoughts. Through its control over the mind, the regenerative tissue cannot find its own strength; therefore, it becomes weaker. The hernia is forced out through the tissue and creates a rupture. The navel area is number one; this is the area where we learn to nourish ourselves; it becomes strangled through the ego completely demanding control.

This yearning is passed on to the next generation through the struggle of the ego not allowing itself its own free rein. There is no loyalty to the self, and, if there is no loyalty, they can never achieve their royalty. Therefore, the next generation has had to accept all these disabilities which have been quietly creating themselves over time. The DNA was following its program, creating the next important step for the next generation to inherit.

Stubbornness genetically set the scene for your father's prostate problems. The first thing the prostate interferes with is the sexual act, where man never feels fully satisfied. The prostate gland – and, remember this is God's land that we are mentioning – is there to act like a guardian, and it should supply the proteins needed to help the ejaculation flow through, to ease the pressure of the sexual act. In other words, he has difficulties in turning himself on, and the fulfilment of the sexual act was not and is not appreciated. It is as though the act is an order of participation; it is not coerced throughout the mind. The ego won't allow it to be fulfilled. It can never be satisfied with its own self-acclaim. Ask your mother; she will verify what I am saying! It is as though the act is over before it even begins! Many women have explained their dilemma to me, and that is why I am repeating their story.

Now we begin to understand how your father set the scene for your testicles to hide inside their insecurity, not wanting to release until you were almost through your teenage years. This was to show you how the weakness was carried through the river of your life, and why the testicle had to create the tear in order for the fluid to gather. The testicle sac is the storehouse of the next generation. Your Law of Self is showing you, step by step, what the family lineage is creating for the next generation to balance on behalf of the whole family tree.

I have not dealt with many men's problems, as they like to keep these to themselves. It is when they bother to enquire to learn about themselves that they open up to finding an answer to their questions. They don't want to know about it, and that is through them supporting themselves with the strength of their inheritance. What was this supreme personality in the beginning? The overriding factor was stubbornness, which is not the creation of their emotional thinking.

Your Notes:

CHAPTER TWENTY FIVE

Thoughts

Our thoughts evolve in the same way as the Fibonacci system has created itself; our positive thoughts build upon themselves. Take a thought and watch how it evolves itself, and you will see how it ends up through the mathematical measuring by the mind. Follow the direction of the thought as to where it is leading itself to, and watch as it explodes and multiplies itself. Energy attracts attention, whether it be positive or negative, remember we reap our own harvest by what we sow.

In order for you to become a healer of your own and others' energy, you must equate your intelligence with and through the unconscious mind. Just make sure you hear your own energy before you begin to help others. As you enter up into this territory, you will hear and clear your patients' force fields, reminding them of their responsibilities and the opportunities that they have to heal themselves.

The pine cone, sunflower, and nautilus shell all are perfect examples of how the Fibonacci sequence builds upon itself. Each one is a collective that harmonizes its own energy. The pine cone is situated at the beginning of the tour through the Vatican; it is shepherded with two peacocks standing on each side of it. Shamanically, they represent the balance of ego and pride. The Fibonacci sequence is a perfect creation of how we must learn to balance our minds. The more our minds are balanced, the more we create a better world for all of us to walk, step by step.

I am writing this story for your ego, or your fear within, to listen to – and also for your trapped emotional mind to hear – in order to gather them together so that you can believe in your next possible moment.

Our Spirituality is the eclectic light that we earn through obeying this intelligence that we refer to as "home"; it is permanently connected throughout every species on this wonderful planet. It is the conscious, subconscious and unconscious minds working as one. There is only one God, and there is only one set of Laws of the Universe – both are refracted in identical unison throughout every cell of our body.

I bow to the Laws of the Universe for sharing with me this opportunity to explain my earnings to you. The next challenge begins in book IV, which explains the word death – that is, why, how, when, and where we earn the codes to accept our final sentience.

Thank you for reading this book through my story.

Your Notes:

Books By O.M. Kelly (Omni)

Decoding The Mind Of God
Author O.M. Kelly's seminal work, "Decoding the Mind of God", is a compilation of nine volumes of metaphysical information based on the research into the coded information of the Laws of the Universe, also known as the Collective Consciousness, and represents a groundbreaking contribution to our understanding of the metaphysical universe. Now, all nine volumes are being released as separate, revised books, each offering a unique perspective on the universe's workings. Omni's work has been widely acclaimed for its depth of insight, and her contributions to the field of metaphysics have been groundbreaking.
The nine separate volumes encompassing:

The Laws of the Universe
Thought
Dis-Ease
Death
Sexuality and Spirituality
The Dolphin's Breath
Sacred Alphabet and Numerology
Sacred Fung Shwa
Extra-Terrestrial Intelligence.
Updated version of each book now being released separately.

Book I. Decoding The Laws Of The Universe
If you're looking to unlock the hidden potential within you and transform your life, "Decoding the Laws of the Universe" is the book for you. This powerful and insightful book is designed to help you understand the deeper, metaphysical aspects of life and tap into the transformative power of the universe utilising the secrets of our Individual Universal Law.

This book serves to introduce you into the secrets of our Individual Universal Law. This amazing knowledge and wisdom, is transformative on a personal level and creates the opportunity for you to interrelate with the Laws of the Universe. Throughout this book, you will dive deep into the inner workings of your mind and discover the hidden laws that govern your life. You will learn about the alchemy of the mind and how to harness its power to create positive change in your life and the world around you. Through the lens of Metaphysical philosophy, you will gain a new perspective on the world and your place in it. You will learn how the universe communicates with you through coded intelligence and how to unlock the hidden messages that are all around you.

This book is a journey for personal transformation and spiritual growth. Take a voyage of exploration of the expansive vistas of information discovering the codes of Metaphysics and the Quest of Life. You will learn the Metaphysical coded wisdom of the ancients for the necessary mind elements to transit into a higher mindset. Explore the secret relationship between the Earth and human beings, the higher mind, the Metaphysical journey, the importance of self, belief in self, the codes of mythology, a higher level of attainment, releasing the past, fears and evolving one's light on a Metaphysical level, what causes stress, work place promotion and why it does not happen, and many other topics. Included is a short overview of the conventional Twelve Laws of the Universe.

Book II. Decoding Thought
Welcome to a journey of self-discovery and exploration of the mysteries of the universe. "Decoding Thought" is a ground-breaking book that explores the power of the mind and the principles of metaphysical thought. Through a deep exploration of the mind and body connection, the author provides readers with insights to unlock the full potential of their thoughts. This book provides a guide to harnessing the power of the mind to create the life you desire. With explanations of metaphysical principles, the book makes these often complex concepts accessible to readers. "Decoding Thought" takes you on a journey through the vast landscape of the human mind. Explore the mysteries of thought power, and how it can shape our reality and transform our lives. The power of thought is not just a theoretical concept. It is a tangible force that can be harnessed to bring about significant changes in our lives.

This book can expand your consciousness and open your mind to new possibilities. By exploring the metaphysical principles that underlie our existence, you can gain a new perspective on life and the world around you. This book provides through a metaphysical interpretation explanations into the various aspects of thought power, including how it is linked to our DNA, and the roles played by the pituitary and pineal glands in our thought processes. O.M. Kelly also explains the metaphysical language in reference to the codes of the Egyptian Philosophies, the Bible, myths, cultures, and how they connect to the power of thought. The journey continues with a deep dive into the inner Secret School of Metaphysics, where we discover the Alchemy of the Brain and the pathway to our truth. Discover the unconscious/higher mind, and our Life Quest, which opens the doors to the Psychometric Consciousness. Through the lens of metaphysical interpretation, you will gain a new perspective on the impact of thought on our mental and emotional states that includes a look at Depression, Coping with Change and how to retrain our brain patterns to be positive and moving forward for our Financial Abundance and manifesting prosperity. The book ends with a brief overview of the brain/mind, and a short Q&A on thought power. This metaphysical book on the power of thought is a guide to discovering your true potential and creating the life you desire.

"Decoding Thought" is a must-read for anyone seeking to unlock the full potential of their mind and harness the power of the universe to create a life of fulfilment and this book serves as an invaluable resource.

Book III. Decoding Dis-Ease

Introducing "Decoding Dis-Ease" a Metaphysical Interpretation into understanding the intricate web of factors that contribute to our health and well-being. From the author of several groundbreaking works on the interaction of the mind and body, this book delves into a wide range of topics related to dis-ease. It is a fascinating and insightful book that offers a fresh perspective on health and healing. It is a must-read for anyone interested in the mind-body connection.

Readers will be inspired to embark on a quest of discovering the codes within themselves, recognizing that every cell in our body is pure Cosmic Consciousness. They will also gain a deeper understanding of specific health topics such as the thyroid, the kidneys, men's problems, and many other topics from a Metaphysical perspective. The book also examines how a dis-ease is given to us in group energy and the complex interplay between our bodies and minds, and how every human has the consequences of all that we do and experience.

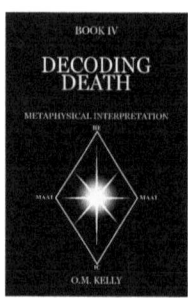

Book IV. Decoding Death

Looking for a thought-provoking exploration of death and the afterlife? Look no further than O.M. Kelly's book, "Decoding Death".

"Decoding Death takes us on a transformative Metaphysical journey through the mysteries of the Universe. O.M. Kelly—known as Omni—provides an expanded horizon of possibilities, awareness, and a transformative perspective. In this book, Omni delves into a wide range of topics related to dying and death, from the loss of a loved one to a viewing of the afterlife. Omni has a unique ability to view the Laws of the Universe using her extraordinary state of heightened awareness and multi-dimensional perception and through the lens of metaphysics offers a unique perspective on the nature of death and what it means for the human experience.

Omni shares personal experiences and stories, including the passing of her late husband, brother, and parents, and offers a metaphysical insight for those dealing with loss and grief. She explores the transformational process of death and the potential for spiritual growth and enlightenment. The book explains that the human experience of death is part of a larger Universal process that is ultimately guided by a higher intelligence referred to as God (Laws of the Universe/Collective Consciousness) or whatever name you prefer. Omni's exploration of death is both metaphysically comprehensive and thought-provoking, offering readers a deep and nuanced understanding of one of life's greatest mysteries. With chapters on the Three Doorways—Three Stages of Death, The Quantum Hologram—Why a partner dies for the other partner to progress in the "Journey of Life", The Passing to the Afterlife, and many other enlightening chapters, "Decoding Death" offers a unique viewpoint. By drawing on a range of religious, philosophical, and metaphysical perspectives, Omni offers a compelling vision of the human experience of death and its role in the larger Universal Law.

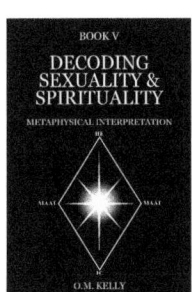

Book V. Decoding Sexuality And Spirituality

Welcome to "Decoding Sexuality and Spirituality" by O.M. Kelly. In this book, explore the fascinating relationship between our sexuality and spirituality, and how these two aspects of ourselves are intimately intertwined. Delve into the concept that sexuality is the doorway to our spirituality, and examine the powerful and transformative energy that is generated when we fully embrace our sexual selves. The book also explores the notion of the metaphysical orgasmic cloud, and how it can be used to deepen our connection to our spiritual selves. We will also examine the role of marriage in our sexual and spiritual lives.

For women, the book offers a unique perspective on the journey of embracing sexuality and spirituality, as well as insights into the different stages of life and how they impact our sexual and spiritual selves. Drawing on both ancient wisdom traditions and metaphysical mythology, the book examines the myth of Hercules and how it relates to our sexual intelligence. By decoding the symbolism of this myth, we can gain a deeper understanding of the ways in which our sexuality and spirituality intersect and influence each other. So if you are ready to embark on a journey of self-discovery and unlock the true potential of your sexual and spiritual selves, then "Decoding Sexuality and Spirituality" is the book for you.

VI. Decoding The Dolphin's Breath

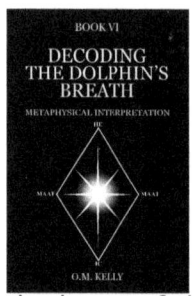

"Decoding The Dolphin's Breath" by O.M. Kelly (Omni) is a captivating exploration of the relationship between humans and dolphins. The book begins with a poignant account of a real-life encounter between the author and a group of wild dolphins, setting the stage for a deep dive into the spiritual and metaphysical significance of dolphins. This captivating book takes readers on a journey into the heart of the dolphin-human relationship, exploring the ways in which these majestic creatures can help us attune to the power of free will, and telepathic communication.

Throughout the Laws of Shamanism the wonderful Dolphin in consciousness, represents the attainment we can reach through ourselves earning our freedom of will. This book explains the benefits of the dolphins breath—the why and how we use the breath that influences our divine mentality. Further, it's a story which reveals how the dolphins have taught us the process to be free of fear, and to tap into the Language of Babylon—to understand the language of Earth. One of the key themes of the book is the idea that dolphins are always breathing their total freedom of thought, and the author provides insights into how humans can learn from this remarkable trait. The book also invites readers to embark on a journey into understanding the telepathic communication of whales and dolphins. Inclusive in the book is a written meditation which assists you to connect to the external consciousness and release the fear that you have wrapped around yourself for protection.

Overall, this book offers a unique and fascinating perspective on the metaphysics of dolphins, and will appeal to anyone interested in spirituality, and the power of the mind.

Book VII. Decoding The Sacred Alphabet And Numerology

This book offers a myriad of explanations concerning the higher consciousness in relationship to names, places and numbers. "Decoding The Sacred Alphabet & Numerology" by O.M. Kelly (Omni) is a thought-provoking and enlightening read that

offers a unique perspective on the metaphysical world of letters and numbers.

Omni's insights and teachings are sure to inspire readers to deepen their understanding of the ancient sacred codes to names of places, your name and the sacred alphabet. The author also delves into the practice of metaphysical numerology, which involves using numerical values to interpret personality traits, life paths, and other aspects of a person's life. Omni explains how metaphysical numerology can be used to gain insight into our spiritual path and to better understand our purpose in life. Your ability to decipher the Sacred Alphabet and Numerology codes commonly and constantly presented to you throughout your life, will open opportunities to expand your consciousness and awareness you never thought possible.

Embark on a journey through the myth of Babylon and Shambhala and discover the sacred language that connects us all. Explore Luxor, the Delta Giza Saqqara and Faiyum, and Solomon's Temple, and uncover the mysteries of Akhenaton and Tomb KV-63. Find out how to unravel the threads of your DNA and unlock the ancient knowledge of the Old Aramaic Story of Aladdin and the Lamp. Explore Grecian stories through the Metaphysical language and travel along the Old Silk Road. Discover the Shamanic inheritance of numbers and their meanings, and learn how we rely on numbers to read the hidden language of the universe. Join O.M. Kelly on a journey of self-discovery and uncover the divine language within.

Book VIII. Decoding Sacred Fung Shwa

Introducing "Decoding Sacred Fung Shwa", the revolutionary guide to understanding and harnessing the energy within your home and yourself. In this book, author O.M. Kelly (Omni), has introduced a metaphysical sixth element that takes our understanding of energy to the next level. By incorporating "Your Life Force," we gain deeper insight into the connection between our homes and our emotional well-being. Discover the power of Fung Shwa and learn how to use it to create a balanced and harmonized environment that supports your mind, body, and Soul.

The book explains the meaning of Sacred Fung Shwa to the Shamanistic principles that underpin it. Delve into the metaphysical medicine wheel and explore the elements of life, before moving on to practical applications of Fung Shwa in the home.

Learn how to visualize your home as a collective energy and clear the clutter to enhance its flow. Discover your Astrological colours and how they can be used in Fung Shwa design, from the kitchen to the bedroom and beyond. Explore the compatibility of personal colours in relationships, and discover the power of paintings, pictures, and mirrors to enhance your home's energy.

But Fung Shwa isn't just about the home—we also explore its applications in the office environment and in small retail businesses. Learn how to apply Fung Shwa principles to a clothing store, shoe store, or café, even discover the role of Fung Shwa in money, and to Metaphysical Numerology.

Throughout it all, we focus on the quest of life and how Fung Shwa can help you achieve your goals and live your best life. So what are you waiting for? Dive into the world of Fung Shwa and transform your home, your business, and your life today!

Book IX. Decoding Extra-Terrestrial Intelligence
Are you ready to embark on a journey of self-discovery? Look no further than O.M. Kelly's groundbreaking book, Book IX "Decoding Extra-Terrestrial Intelligence". Through metaphysical interpretation, O.M. Kelly (Omni) has unlocked the secrets of the universe and revealed that the key to our next step in human evolution lies within ourselves. This book will show you how to tap into the indelible imprint of holographic importance that is seeded within every human, and unleash the Extra-Terrestrial Intelligence that resides within you. Omni shares her own personal journey of encountering Beings of Light and how it has transformed her understanding of the universe and humanity's place within it.

Omni presents the concept that we all have Extra-Terrestrial Intelligence, and have the ability to tap into the vast knowledge and secrets of the universe. The ancient civilizations left behind clues and teachings about this metaphysical existence and it is up to us to continue to uncover and advance the way we think. Through this journey of life, we can unlock the secrets of our own consciousness and tap into the full potential of our existence. This is a fascinating exploration of the mysteries of the universe and the potential for our own personal evolution.

Readers who are interested in self-transformation through universal truths, Metaphysical exploration for personal growth and a journey of self-discovery would be interested in reading this insightful book on contact with Beings of Light and Extra-terrestrial Intelligence, exploring ancient civilizations and the knowledge they possessed about the universe and the human mind.

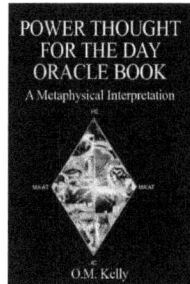

Power Thought for the Day Oracle Book

"Power Thought For The Day Oracle Book" provides insights to assist you on your life path. Through the "Totem" energy of all, the ancient species that have evolved before us, represent an emotional inheritance that we can rely on to sustain the moment. Each species that has evolved on this planet is recorded into our cellular memory. This book with 22 Major Arcana Shamanic Power Animal Totems provides a contemporary metaphysical interpretation symbolic of our evolution. By selecting a page of the book the Shamanic animal will provide an insight in how you are thinking at this moment in time. Through the contemporary Laws of Shamanism (with a metaphysical interpretation), O.M. Kelly (Omni) has produced a book that will assist the "Path of the Initiate" in emotional intelligence when our mind is in the field of doubt. When we become aware of how we are thinking it is a catalyst for transformation. This compact little book is a handy 4 x 7 inches or 10.2 x 17.8 cm to fit into your pocket or handbag.

How to use the book:
Our higher mind has no time; it steps into and works on behalf of the thought of the moment. This book encompasses 22 Major Totem Power representations, symbolic of our evolution. Close your eyes and inhale and exhale a deep breath and relax and allow yourself no thought as you select the right page of the Shamanic animal presented in this book. The right page will always appear for you at the right moment and you will discover how the power animals are working with you for insight into their wisdom. Different power animals come into our lives at various phases offering messages to guide us on our path.

Decoding the Shaman Within

In "Decoding the Shaman Within" international author O.M. Kelly (Omni) shares her Shamanic metaphysical journey. It would be termed a contemporary Shamanic initiation journey; a powerful spiritual enlightenment and transformational voyage of discovering the codes of Metaphysics and the Quest of Life. Through the sacred passage of time Omni discovered the secret codes of the Collective Consciousness (Laws of the Universe) to trek a higher level of consciousness. Throughout

Omni's training to receive the breath of Shamanism, many Elders from other cultures came to Australia and initiated her into their own tribal laws. Most of these Elders were men who arrived on Omni's doorstep uninvited but had received the call from the Universe to pass on their knowledge. Those magnificent people who had also earned their Shamanic experiences, only stayed long enough to give Omni their gift of consciousness and to initiate her into a new Shamanic name, which their tribe had bestowed, and then they disappeared out of Omni's life as quickly as they had come into it.

The Shamanic path in a Metaphysical perspective is the oldest pathway of the tribal law through the evolution of humanity. The Shaman is trained in the ancient language that is instilled in every genetic code that humanity carries within their DNA; you either have the opportunity to open it up and use it, or you just don't bother and choose to ignore it! It is as simple as that!

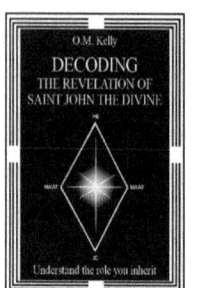

Decoding the Revelation of Saint John the Divine: Understand the role you inherit

The amazing breakthrough book "Decoding the Revelation of Saint John the Divine: Understand the role you inherit", is for anyone with an open, inquiring mind, seeking answers to the surreal descriptions of Earth's final days.

Through years of research O.M. Kelly interprets the cryptology behind the codes of mythology and various religions and has Metaphysically interpreted how the Holy Bible had been written through the original codex of Egyptology. The biblical stories were collected and condensed through the educated minds of that time.

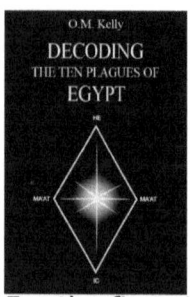

Decoding the Ten Plagues of Egypt

"Decoding the Ten Plagues of Egypt" presents a fresh insight into understanding the hidden structure of the language of how the Bible was written. The reader is introduced to the step by step Metaphysical decoding of the mystifying language, regarding the plagues from the Book of Exodus, Chapters: 7-12 in the Bible.

For the first time in contemporary history the essence of the Book of Exodus and its previously unsolved intriguing language will be revealed to provide deeper knowledge and clearer perception to unlock the significance the Book of Exodus is explaining to us.

Decoding Dreams

In "Decoding Dreams" international author O.M. Kelly (Omni), introduces a metaphysical interpretation of the dreams we dream. At times, we may believe that dreams allow us to peer into another world. O.M. Kelly provides the codes for us to understand that other world of dreams—or, through the Shamanic Principles, our "Vision Worlds". Dreams are created through your unconscious/higher mind communicating back to you; dreams are reminding you of the lessons that you need to understand regarding yourself. You cannot hear them if your mind is filled with incessant chatter. The ego refuses to conform when it is in control of the moment. Dreams can range from a pleasant dream, which could be a recommendation to add to what you are doing, to a nightmare, which is a wake-up call from your higher self regarding what you are doing to yourself. As you read this book, keep in mind that learning to metaphysically interpret your dreams is a step-by-step process. Areas covered in the book are: Dream Representations (Animal Kingdom and the Human Kingdom), Questions and Answers about Dreams, and Dream Interpretations.

Reprint coming in the near future.

www.ingramcontent.com/pod-product-compliance
Lightning Source LLC
Chambersburg PA
CBHW062039290426
44109CB00026B/2670